Oriental Rugs

An Updated Guide

Revised 2ⁿᵈ Edition

Charles W. Jacobsen

with
Bruce E. Kitney
and the staff of Charles W. Jacobsen, Inc.

Copyright ® 1977, 1983 by Charles W. Jacobsen, Inc.

Revised Edition
First Published in 1977 by Charles W. Jacobsen, Inc.

Published by
Charles W. Jacobsen, Inc.
401 South Salina Street
Syracuse, New York

Printed in the United States of America by Eastwood Litho, Inc., Syracuse, New York

TABLE OF CONTENTS

LIST OF ILLUSTRATIONS

LIST OF ILLUSTRATIONS

(Continued)

PREFACE

My last effort as an author was in 1977 when ORIENTAL RUGS - AN UP-DATED GUIDE was completed and published. There had been so many changes in the rug world in the 1970's that a small book providing up-to-date information seemed essential. The reaction to the UPDATED GUIDE was very favorable and extremely gratifying. We have always felt that for interest in Oriental rugs to grow the general public must be given correct information about them. The old days when rug dealers could rely on fanciful stories instead of real knowledge are thankfully long gone.

Of course, change in the world did not stop in 1977. In the years since the UPDATED GUIDE appeared, developments have occurred which affect the availability and price of many rug types and these developements need to be called to the attention of those interested in Oriental rugs new or old.

With this in mind we felt it time to issue a rewritten and expanded second edition of ORIENTAL RUGS - AN UPDATED GUIDE. My big book, ORIEN-TAL RUGS - A COMPLETE GUIDE contains a great deal of information about Oriental rugs woven up to about 1970. This rug encyclopedia has enjoyed world-wide distribution and is of value for all rug types woven during the past hundred years. Used together with the COMPLETE GUIDE, this new UPDATED GUIDE should be of great assistance to both dealer and rug enthusiast. This present book is intended as a practical guide, outlining the facts about rugs as we know them. Read about rugs, buy them and collect them . . . but most of all, live with them and enjoy them.

Charles W Jacobsen

PART I
CHAPTER ONE
IN GENERAL

The changes in the Oriental rug situation are still greater today than they were when the first edition of the UPDATED GUIDE was written. We pointed out the fact that the Iran of the 1970's had become so rich under the Shah with its fifty million dollar a day income from oil that weaving wages had risen from about a dollar a day to five dollars a day. The price of rugs from Iran was so inflated that they were not competitive in cost with Oriental rugs from areas where labor costs were lower. By the late 1970's three-fourths of our sales were rugs from India, Pakistan, and Rumania. Since the abdication of the Shah we have practically eliminated new Iranian rugs from our stock except for a few very fine Nains, Isphahans, silk Qums, and a few extra fine Bijars. There are Iranian rugs in the hands of some dealers and a good number in the stock of some importers in New York and in Germany and London, but with prices so high they are not selling readily.

When the hostages were taken at the American Embassy in 1979 there were over $150,000,000 worth of Iranian rugs in Tehran alone, all of these at tremendously inflated prices. Trade with Iran was embargoed for more than a year and this further reduced the availability of Iranian rugs. With the final release of the United States' diplomatic personnel, relations with Iran calmed, but currency restrictions, customs requirements, and continuing disruptions in Iran meant that the export of Iranian rugs has not yet recovered to pre-revolution levels. With Iran eliminated as a source of rugs, other areas quickly moved to fill the void.

RUGS FROM INDIA - India has now become a major source for most types of rugs, producing many more rugs than Iran. After World War I and up until ten or fifteen years ago most of the Indian production was in two types: various Chinese designs, and French Savonnerie and Aubusson designs. Both types came in many qualities from crude, inferior rugs with fifteen to twenty-five knots per square inch to very excellent carpets. Today some of the best and most beautiful rugs available are being made in India in excellent quality. Many of these are rugs employing famous old Persian designs. Comparatively few of the Savonnerie and Aubusson types are made today. The Indian weavers do not want to produce these types for it is more profitable to make rugs in Persian designs.

The quality of the best of these Indian rugs in Iranian designs is outstanding. We can specify the quality of wool used, the number of knots to the inch, and even the thickness of the pile. To illustrate, several years ago a long time friend and rug expert from London visited our showroom. We laid two 9 x 12 ft. Sarabend rugs side by side for him to examine. One was from Iran and cost about $4,000 wholesale which meant, of course, that it had to be sold for about $6,000 at retail. The other rug was from India. After carefully inspecting both rugs this expert judged the Indian rug to be superior in all respects to the Sarabend from Iran. Later he wrote us that, "From my experience the Indian and Pakistani carpets they are making now, in good designs and fine quality, are better than Persian."

RUGS FROM RUMANIA - There are changes as well affecting rugs from Rumania, not so much in quality or beauty as in popularity or "saleability." Beginning some ten years ago we began to find some of the most beautiful new rugs we had ever seen among the Rumanian rugs we examined. The Rumanians wove famous old Persian designs in such exquisite soft colors that they looked more antique than some old rugs. One must remember that more than half of the rugs that came from Iran between 1905 and 1965 were both chemically bleached and redyed ("washed and painted" in the trade). This washing and painting process was an attempt to overcome the harsh, bright colors found in most new rugs from Iran. The Rumanian rugs were not bleached and redyed and yet the colors were soft and the designs traditional. Today the standard qualitiy rugs from Rumania cost as much as the finest and best rugs from India like the best of the Sarouks, Tabriz, and Isphahans which are heavier, more finely woven, and have superior wool. As beautiful as they are, Rumanian rugs have been hurt by the price advantage of the Indian rugs and the best of the Indians are actually superior rugs. Rumanian rugs are good looking and durable but importers like us will find difficulty in selling them at the same price as the best of the rugs from India. We hope the market will adjust and that rugs from Rumania will become the value they should be.

RUGS FROM TURKEY - We are getting more exquisite, excellent quality rugs in the old designs from Turkey than we have had in fifty years. There are several general qualities we like, among them the Kula and Basmachi grades. Many of the village rugs from Turkey are woven in the traditional way on woolen warp and weft. For the most part these rugs have strong geometric designs. Colors are rich but soft; earth tones including rust, green, gold, and blue are common. There are also extremely fine wool, wool/silk, and all silk rugs available from Turkey. The best of the silk Turkish rugs woven today are among the finest Oriental rugs ever made anywhere. These pieces are expensive but their quality is magnificent. If someone were beginning a collection of good rugs available in today's market they would certainly consider some of the Turkish types.

CHINESE RUGS - When Colonel Jacobsen wrote his COMPLETE GUIDE in the 1960's there were no Chinese rugs to speak of available in America, because with China a communist country import duty was very high -- 45% as compared with 11% from other "most favored nation" trading partners. Ten or fifteen years ago some very excellent Chinese rugs were to be seen in the bonded ware-houses in London but we did not buy them because we would not pay the 45% duty. Now we are on more friendly terms with China and the duty has been reduced to only 5% -- the lowest rate in over sixty years.

In the past few years we have seen many ads in the New York papers for Chinese rugs. Most of these are superb rugs, the so-called "90 line" quality. In the 9 x 12 ft. size most were advertised for $4,000 and up. These were good rugs but we did not consider them very saleable at such a price. We know that the sales so advertised in New York failed badly. In the recent past the New York market has been flooded with Chinese rugs, not only the 90 line grade but lesser qualities (that are still good rugs) and a medium quality in antique design and finish that is, in our opinion, very good value. Be sure that in the near future there will continue to be great numbers of Chinese rugs available. These will vary anywhere from mediocre to superior quality. We also expect to find the Chinese producing Persian designs just as India has, and they will probably produce them in a variety of grades. The big question is how expensive these rugs from China will be.

RUGS FROM AFGHANISTAN - Buying trips to Afghanistan ended when the Russians occupied the country. Still there are good numbers of small Afghans to be had, some of them first going to the London market and then coming to the United States. Some excellent rugs in carpet sizes are available as well, along with some superb scatters with very fine knot counts woven on silk warp and weft.

For most weaving areas the big change in the last few years is the general reduction in United States' customs duty on rugs to only 5%. When our company was founded in 1924 import duty on rugs from all weaving areas was 45%, and on small mats 55%. During the Depression duty was not less than fifty cents a square foot. It is also the case that our American dollar has strengthened against other currencies making rugs we import cost somewhat less due to this favorable rate of exchange. The selection of rug types available today has never been larger. Many of these rugs come from countries where labor costs remain low making them excellent values. For the knowledgeable buyer there are many choice and beautiful Oriental rugs available today . . . and at least as important, these rugs are available at reasonable cost.

CHAPTER TWO
RUGS FROM IRAN

Perhaps the greatest change of all affecting the rug business since World War II is the fact that Iranian rugs have practically ceased to be available, at least in any number. For over a hundred years two-thirds of all handmade Orientals sold the world over -- and especially in America -- came from Iran. The takeover of the U. S. Embassy in 1979 ended the export of rugs from Iran to the United States for over a year and drastically changed the make-up of most dealers' inventories. Many of the small dealers around the country still own some Iranian rugs as a part of their stock, but these are rugs almost invariably bought at over-inflated prices. A few of the largest U. S. importers with family connections in Iran still have stocks of Iranian rugs in New York but they are at such high prices that few will be sold. Most of these rugs will have to be disposed of by giving them to auctioneers with the hope that some will find buyers. Others will have to be bundled up and shipped off to dealers who conduct "sales" around the country at department stores which do not have permanent Oriental rug departments. Again most all the Iranian rugs we have seen advertised at such sales during the past several years have been offered at unrealistically high prices. With almost no rugs coming from Iran many importers and small dealers have been practically dormant in the last few years because they did not plan ahead.

For several years before the abdication of the Shah we were down-grading rugs from Iran because of two things: the deterioration of quality of most types and the inflated prices asked for them. It has been our experience that few customers will buy an Iranian rug if they find, as they can, a rug of similar design in equal or better quality from India or Pakistan or Rumania for a fraction of the price of the Iranian rug.

In the mid-1970's Iranian rugs were offered at prices based upon an inflated cost of labor. Since the early 1960's the Shah worked to develop Iran into an industrialized nation. Hundreds of companies from the west opened offices and plants in Tehran and other Persian cities. All of this investment caused tremendous inflation in the country and in the cities wages rose from fifty cents or a dollar a day to three, four, or five dollars per day. A million people left their farms and villages and came to Tehran to look for work at these high wages. Instead of weaving at home people deserted the looms because they hoped to earn more in the cities. Unfortunately most of the people found they did not have the skills to find work in the new factories and plants. By the mid-1970's shanty towns ringed many Iranian cities and the poor people living in these slums listened to the promises of those who wanted to overthrow the Shah. With so much inflation, rugs naturally went higher and higher in price, and finally became so expensive that dealers would not buy them because they could not sell them to their customers.

For several years before the abdication of the Shah we could not have existed with our large staff and with sufficient volume of sales had we depended upon sales from Iranian rugs alone. We sold a good number of rugs from Iran but it dwindled with each succeeding year. By 1980 the rugs from the Hamadan dis- trict--the many types such as Bibicabad, Hosseinabad, Dergazine, Kazvin, and Ingelas--had practically disappeared from the market. They were not being made in numbers and could not be sold at the prices asked. Before they ceased coming, the Ingelas was one of the more tightly woven of the types--perhaps the best of the

4

Hamadan group. By 1979 the average Ingelas rug was about half the knottage per square inch as before and some of them were very coarse indeed. The lovely, inexpensive Bibicabad, many with nice soft colors, disappeared completely from the American market. They too had cheapened in quality. The best of the floral rugs from the Hamadan district was the Kazvin. Once woven in greater numbers, they practically disappeared by about 1970. For several years it was hard to find one as good as those made in the 50's and early 60's. In those years we could go to any New York importer and find forty or fifty big Kazvins, 10 x 14ft. to 12 x 20ft., lined up against the wall. Literally hundreds would be available to choose among. They first came in a colorful red field but finally most were made with the ivory open field on the order of a Kirman. Quality deteriorated badly but the prices went higher and higher.

The same is true of rugs from the Sarouk district. A few of the Sarouks continued to come in the typical modern, allover floral design with red background. These rugs were made with the idea that they would be chemically washed and painted when they arrived in America. It was about 1965 when this practice ended as the large plants in Jersey City, Garden City, and on Long Island went out of the chemical washing and painting business. Until then almost all of the Sarouks imported from about 1905 had been both chemically washed and painted. We never sold washed and painted Sarouks and Colonel Jacobsen wrote many articles denouncing this practice.

From the great weaving district around Arak where all of the Sarouks were made also came the Araks, Mahals, Sultanabads, and Muskabads; the last being the cheapest quality rugs. We called all the old, lovely carpet size rugs from this district Sultanabad. These were attractive and very inexpensive rugs which sold in the 1950's for $395 to $850 for the cheapest in the 10 x 14ft. size. Today one of these rugs would undoubtedly cost $1,500 and more at wholesale and few of them have come on the market lately.

The great Tabriz district furnished many exquisite rugs beginning about 1950. Tabriz rugs made before the turn of the century were generally all very fine quality, but beginning about 1920 and up through the Depression and World War II there appeared on the market many groups of mediocre rugs, most of them semi-antique and some even antique, and all very inexpensive. One producer in Tabriz did furnish to a small importer some very fine Tabriz during the Depression at about $8.00 a square foot wholesale, a price which was to high to be saleable at that time.

Along in the 1950's appeared the Taba-Tabaie Tabriz in soft earth tones and in lovely old designs. These quickly became the most popular Iranian rugs available, even taking many of the Kirman sales as they were chosen over the Kirman by people who wanted light colors. Thousands of Tabriz came and they sold even at high prices. A few will be sold today in isolated places.

Unfortunately in the four or five years before the end of the Shah these rugs were cheapened in quality even as the prices went higher. Colonel Jacobsen and two officers of our company inspected more than a hundred Tabriz rugs from one of the largest importers in New York, a source from whom we had bought a good many rugs in the past. Bale after bale of Tabriz rugs were opened and without exception the rugs were coarser and harsher in color than they had been before.

The same Tabriz district is the marketplace for the well known Herez type which included the Herez itself along with Gorevan, Mehriban, Bakshaish, Ahar, and other associated types. The Herez type in many qualities has been popular in this country for more than 80 years. In the past Herez were among the least expensive rugs available. The best and loveliest of the antiques were truly attractive rugs and remain so today. The thousands of these that we sold for $195 to $495 in the 9 x 12ft. size were perhaps the greatest values ever offered among rugs from Iran. But today Iranian Herez rugs are not saleable from our point of view at current prices. How could a good average quality rug like this be sold for so much? The last we bought cost nearly $20 a square foot. We sold several in the 9 x 12ft. size for $2,500 and made almost no profit on them. At the same time we had Herez rugs from India in antique designs and antique colors which were of equal if not better quality that we could sell at retail (and at a good profit!) for $1,600 to $1,700. Colonel Jacobsen was amazed when one of the large importers called offering a new shipment of Herez rugs from Iran at wholesale price of $25 to $35 a square foot, meaning a cost of $3,000 at wholesale for a 9 x 12ft. Herez. These prices strike us as tremendously inflated.

We received a brochure from the State Department which is sent to banks and other institutions with the idea of encouraging wealthy individuals to purchase and donate furnishings for the government's use. Illustrated were two Herez rugs, one large one at about $9,500 and one about 8 x 11 at $4,500! We liked the Herez but we doubt if many customers who see what is available from India and Rumania in the Herez motif would buy the Iranian rug at two or three times the price when the rugs from these countries in most cases would be more attractive and of better quality.

We could point out many other examples of types which are either not available or not competitive in today's market. A few years ago we inspected five bales of Ardebil rugs from Iran as they were opened at one wholesaler in a New York showroom. This is a rug that was a very popular replacement for the higher priced Caucasian types. For a good many years we had been able to select some excellent Ardebils. From among the hundred rugs we examined, there was not one that our officers liked well enough to buy. They were in a poorer quality than we had been buying and the colors were not right; and yet prices were much higher than they had been. No one would buy one of these Ardebils when we can find a Turkish rug in Kazak or Cabistan design. While Turkish rugs are not cheap, they cost less than the Ardebil and are superior in materials and workmanship.

One other rug type might be mentioned--the Karaja runner. These geometric design runners have been popular in America as an inexpensive but durable runner ever since the 1920's. Many of these rugs from Iran came as semi-antique until about ten or fifteen years ago. Here is an example: in New York at Colonel Jacobsen's oldest and favorite importer's showroom he and his assistants selected forty Karaja runners out of a large new shipment. As they examined them one by one for flaws they discovered that 25 out of the 40 were so crooked and irregular in shape that they could not be used in a hall or on stairs. Now from India there are rugs in the Karaja design made in good numbers and almost every one of them will be almost perfectly straight. If one does vary it is seldom by more than a half inch from one end to the other. They are thicker and superior in weave to the Karajas that have come from Iran in the last ten years (although some of the older Karajas made between 1950 and 1960 were very lovely).

Now that we have discouraged you from looking at Iranian rugs we must point out that a few types available from Iran (although at very high prices) are truly remarkable rugs. The fine Nain and the Isphahan with silk warp and with some 450 to 600 hand tied knots per square inch are as choice as many museum pieces. If the prices on these types were adjusted downward anyone who could afford to do so should buy one.

It is sad to note Iran, the cradle of rug weaving for hundreds of years, pass from the scene at least for the time being. Still, no one can tell what the future will bring. Some few rugs have come to America from Iran during the past years, most brought out through Germany. Some rugs have continued to be shipped if only because some importers with family members in Iran want to get their money out of the country. It is hard to see how many customers will buy Iranian rugs at today's market prices. In our opinion they have to come down half or more before they can compete with types from other areas now available. One must remember that the fact that a rug was woven in Iran is no guarantee of quality.

The greatest number of rugs from Iran came from the Hamadan weaving district and the Herez district but the Hamadans of the last 20 years have been average quality rugs at best; many would call them mediocre. They were practical rugs and lasted well but there are better values available now. In the old days we could find pile after pile of semi-antique Hamadans and could select the most beautiful of these rugs for our stock. We can never forget the early days when we bought hundreds of antique Bahktiaris and Kurds, rugs woven by nomadic tribesmen who wandered with their flocks. Today most of these peoples are settled in villages and for the last 40 years their rugs have been uninspiring for the most part.

Always remember the fact that rugs by the same name will vary greatly as to weave, as to wool quality, as to beauty, and, therefore, as to price. Yet it is our strong opinion that in spite of the changes in Iran, there are more beautiful and better quality Oriental rugs available at moderate prices today than at any time in the last thirty years.

CHAPTER THREE
RUGS FROM INDIA

Far reaching changes have occurred in the Indian rug market in the last twenty years. There have been important changes in the last ten years. Many retail dealers have only become aware of developments in India in the recent past. Our company was among the first to see the possibilities. While India has furnished large quantities of rugs to America, England, and to the world since World War II, types, designs, and qualities available have changed dramatically. India has truly filled the void left by the absence of Iranian rugs. Today the Indian weavers produce rugs in the image of most every Iranian type. Often their carpets are better and prettier rugs than the Iranian rugs they replace. We ourselves buy more than a million dollars' worth of rugs from India each year.

The difference between the situation in India and the situation in Iran can be illustrated by the experience of one of the biggest producers of Iranian Kirman rugs, a man who owned the looms in fifty villages in Iran and shipped thousands of Kirmans to America. Shortly before the abdication of the Shah he told us, "I will probably never make any more rugs. My warehouse is full of half finished rugs. I was paying the weavers a dollar and finally three dollars a day, now they want five dollars. They come in and tell me they won't finish the rugs unless I pay them five dollars a day." What chance did he have when in India we can make almost any Iranian design in any quality we wish to contract for. We can specify the quality of the wool, the number of knots per square inch, and the thickness of the completed rug.

On the whole Indian weavers do a better job than their Iranian counterparts; at least the rugs from India do not have the faults that many of the new Iranian rugs had. At least a third of most types from Iran had some faults, the main problem being the irregularity in shape. Sometimes there would be changes in color in the field and in the design as well.

Orientals from India as from other weaving areas can vary greatly as to quality and beauty and hence as to value. For instance we have available several types of Sarouk from India; the least expensive one is a good heavy rug. It does not have as many knots per square inch as the best but it is as good looking and durable as many florals from Iran and such a Sarouk costs less than a new Iranian Hamadan or Sultanabad. There are Sarouks for which we contract that are superb carpets, better than the majority of Sarouks from Iran woven during the last thirty years. The same is true of Kashan rugs. There are inexpensive Kashans from India that look like and may be mistaken for a much more costly Iranian Kashan. We contract for other qualities of Kashan as well. The finest is more tightly knotted and with better wool than the average Iranian Kashan which wholesales for between $50 and $80 a square foot. Yes, a weaving wage of a dollar a day makes this difference. Always remember that we do not fix the daily wage. We contract for the rug at so much per square meter and the Indian government determines the wage paid to the rug weavers.

In India we contract through suppliers who have many cottages weaving for them. Each cottage has one or more looms and the supplier provides the weavers with a graph for the design of the rug and with the required quantity of wool in the right colors. India, of course, is a poor nation. The average yearly wage is estimated to be about $160.00. However, anyone who travels around India and especially through the Bhadohi district in the area of Varanasi will not fail to note that the weavers in thousands of cottages in the rug making district are better off than people in many other districts of the country.

A SHORT HISTORY OF INDIAN RUGS

Rugs have been woven in India for the last two or three hundred years, but not on the same commercial basis as they have been in Iran. In the 1920's one company imported to the United States small quantities of rugs in the image of Sarouks, Sarabends, and Kirmans. They did not compare with the rugs being woven in India today. Just before World War II one importer had a good number of exquisite large carpets made, pieces equal in weave and quality to the best Iranian Kashans. Most of these pieces were in the old Fereghan design and all of the rugs were in large dimensions. However, most of the Orientals that came to the markets from India after World War I were rugs in the image of the old French Savonneries or were pieces in two or three Chinese designs. A British firm even produced great rolls of plain broadloom, hand woven, in two or three qualities and in a half dozen pastel colors. This wall-to-wall carpet which came in rolls from nine feet to eighteen feet wide did not sell readily but it was beautiful and extra durable. We still see in some homes this wall-to-wall capeting that we sold thirty or more years ago.

Gradually these plain rugs were discontinued and replaced with the French Savonnerie and the pastel Chinese design. Importers in the New York market have brought in great numbers of these rugs over the years, each design and each quality having its own trade name. We entered this market ourselves many years ago and began sending our officers to India every few months. Rugs in French design from India remain popular but are made in less quantity than formerly simply because the Indian weavers prefer to make rugs in Persian patterns—they are in greater demand and hence more profitable. One can order almost any quality he wishes but, of course, the more knottage per square inch and the better the wool the more costly the rug. In the decade from 1970 to 1980 one or two importers in New York brought in millions of dollars worth of very low grade rugs in Savonnerie and Chinese designs. In two or three years there were dozens of pages of ads in the New York newspapers touting these low grade rugs. A whole page costing $10,000 to $12,000 would appear advertising these rugs at very low prices—$395 to $495 for the 9 x 12ft. size. Unfortunately they were not very good rugs and this experience probably hurt the development of the Indian market. These rugs sold because of price only but it is hard to understand how anybody would not recognize them for the coarse and inferior quality rugs they were.

Getting a stock from India is different from buying rugs in Iran or elsewhere. In Iran one would buy from ready stock in the bazaar or warehouse. The buyer examines the completed rug for color, design, and quality and purchases only those rugs that please him in all particulars. In India one contracts for rugs, and many times the rug does not turn out to be quite the quality or quite the colors expected even though weave and colors were carefully specified. In India it is not simply a matter of paying the money and receiving the goods. More often it takes several years of changing colors, wools, and designs before the rug seems just right.

There is general improvement each year, though, in Indian weaving. Certainly India is the main source of Oriental rugs at a price that the public will pay. Today, with our government trying to help these low-standard-of-livng countries, the U. S. import duty is at the lowest level in recent history. Taking all economic developments into account, there is little question that Indian rugs are the best values to be found in today's market.

One could write a book on the subject of rugs from India alone. India is a huge country and with its great population is not likely to become more highly industrialized soon, but with the passage of time the standard of living in India will improve and Indian rugs will cost much more. For years dealers thought no one could weave as well as the Iranians but it is a fact that the Indian weavers can do a better job on many types than the Iranians did. Rug production in India is expanding and in years to come we expect to see even more variety of types and even better quality rugs than are available at present.

CHAPTER FOUR
RUGS FROM PAKISTAN

When Colonel Jacobsen wrote the COMPLETE GUIDE Bokharas from Pakistan were available in limited numbers in the America market in two qualities, the lesser "Lahore" and the better "Karachi" quality (both qualities were actually woven in and around the city of Lahore). The production of rugs in Pakistan has been greatly expanded in the last twenty years and at the same time the rugs themselves have been improved greatly. Most of the rugs that formerly came to the United States were in the less expensive Lahore quality. Some of these still go to the European markets but most of the rugs made for America today are in the heavy Karachi grade. In recent years there have been available finely woven, closely clipped Bokharas with weaves between 200 and 300 knots per square inch. Pakistan with its 80 million population is unlike oil rich Iran. Pakistan is a poor country with a great pool of labor and even today weaving wages are fairly low. The best of the Karachi quality Bokharas, the type we traditionally favor, are thick, tightly woven rugs. These are some of the best quality rugs to be had at any price today. A Karachi grade Bokhara actually costs less than half as much as an Iranian rug of equal weave--and frankly not too many of the Iranian rugs are of equal quality.

Almost all of these rugs from Pakistan come in the typical "Tekke Bokhara" design (see Plate 16), a pattern first used in old Turkoman rugs woven by the Turkoman tribes in central Asia for hundreds of years. Most of the first Bokharas from Pakistan were in some shade of wine or mahogany red. Today these rugs come in many exquisite shades of rust, soft rusty rose, orange-red, and ivory. Some few also have navy or even green backgrounds. Karachi quality rugs are available in many sizes from small mats to giant carpets and in runners up to 20 ft. long. To get these fine quality Karachi rugs, it is usually necessary to contract for them and to wait for the eight to ten months it takes to weave them. One cannot usually go to Pakistan and buy large numbers of them in the market ready made. A buyer can find some selection of the Lahore quality rugs which are woven by families and brought to the market to sell. The Lahore rugs are not as tightly woven as the Karachis nor are they as thick as a rule. In addition they do not employ the very superior wool that is found in the good Karachi quality. Colors are also more limited with most of the Lahore Bokharas having red or cream backgrounds. These all handmade Lahore grade rugs actually cost less than many copies made by machine in this design. For the interested layman we give the following technical details about rug production in Pakistan:

"Lahore" quality Bokhara: 8/14 double ply wool yarn (112 knots per sq. in.) medium to good wool.
8/12 double ply wool yarn (96 knots per sq. in.) coarse to medium wool.

"Karachi" quality Bokhara: 9/18 double ply wool yarn (162 knots per sq. in.) fine wool.
9/16 double ply wool yarn (144 knots per sq. in.) fine wool.
9/14 double ply wool yarn (126 knots per sq. in.) medium to fine wool.

Note: "8/14" means eight horizontal knots and fourteen vertical knots per square inch, or 112 knots per square inch.

Fine quality "London," "Karachi," or "Mauri" Bokharas and rugs in Persian designs:

"Bokhara" designs: Tekke, Youmud, Ersari patterns;	12/24 single ply wool, 288 knots per sq. in. fine wool.
some Kafkazi or Caucasian designs:	12/22 single ply wool, 264 knots per sq. in. fine wool.

Persian floral designs: Kashan, Isphahan, Tabriz, etc. These are the most expensive of the rugs made in Pakistan.	18/20 - 360 knots per sq. in. 16/18 - 288 knots per sq. in. 13/15 - 195 knots per sq. in. 12/14 - 168 knots per sq. in.	All these weaves may have single or double ply wool pile. All are woven with very fine select wool.

Most all fine Bokhara rugs and the finely woven Persian design rugs are produced by contract only. The German buyers have spent incredible amounts of money for these rugs since the 1950's. Contract rugs are woven in so called "factories," actually small thatched roof adobe-walled workshops with looms, washing facilities, and finishing areas. The Lahore qualities are produced outside the cities in private dwellings.

The great news from Pakistan is the appearance of finely woven rugs in Persian designs. Kashan, Sarouk, and Isphahan patterns are most common. These fine rugs from Pakistan are often technically better than Iranian rugs of the same types in that they use superior wool and finer weave and yet still cost less than the Iranian! The difficulty lies in getting sufficient quantities and in arranging for the right sizes.

Pakistan also makes rugs in the image of Caucasian types. These pieces in Kazak, Cabistan, Shirvan, and other designs are called "Kafkazi" -- the Iranian word for Caucasian.

Young (and some not so young!) customers continually ask what rug represents the best value in today's market. Of course, no absolute answer is possible since different people have different requirements and are attracted by different colors and patterns, but we think if any rug type should be considered a 9/18 Karachi Bokhara should be placed near the top of the list. Most Americans prefer a thick, heavy carpet and a 9/18 Bokhara is a tightly woven rug with a good heavy pile of fine wool. Most Europeans on the other hand prefer the very fine thin Bokhara in preference to the thicker Karachi. These tightly woven, closely clipped Bokharas might be of 10/20 quality (200 knots per sq. in.) or in some cases as fine as 12/24 (288 knots per sq. in). It has been our experience, however, that the Bokhara with thicker pile gives better service. For more information please see the entry under "Bokharas" in the alphabetic listing of types in Part II.

CHAPTER FIVE
RUGS FROM TURKEY
(Sometimes identified as "Anatolian rugs" or rugs from Asia Minor)

For over fifty years most dealers have downgraded and disparaged new Turkish rugs, this even though the old Turkish pieces woven prior to World War I were among the most sought after and most expensive of scatter size rugs. We not only disliked the many small prayer rugs woven after World War I but also the large carpets in Iranian design known as "Spartas" and "Anatolians" and by hundreds of other trade names. In the 1920's and 30's these crude, cheap, garish rugs flooded into the wholesale market. We bought none of them and feared that the craftsmanship and artistry of Turkish weavers was lost forever. Fortunately there is very much better news to report now. In the 1970's there began to appear scatter size village rugs from Turkey–rugs in sizes from about 2½ x 6 to 5 x 8 ft. Most were good to very good quality rugs; some were superb. Many were in rich but not gaudy colors. One has to select carefully but we do find pieces in most all the well known designs familiar from among the pre-World War I Turkish types. There are also some runners available and a limited number of carpet size rugs in Oushak, Hereke, and other designs. The quality in most is good but not all designs are as effective as the classic patterns some weavers used. Of course, a weaver need not necessarily make his rug in one of the old designs to make the piece saleable, but some of the new patterns do not seem as pleasing as those refined by time. Certainly the traditional designs of the Melez, Ladik, Bergamo, and Ghiordes types and others are more popular and saleable than some other motifs now available. There is also the problem of some importers who identify rugs as "Melez" or "Ladik" or "Bergamo" which have no resemblance whatsoever to older rugs in these traditional types. The pieces in classic designs, however, are indeed beautiful rugs. They can be placed in the same room, even beside, museum quality Turkish rugs of the 19th century.

The village rugs we like best are for the most part pieces in the Kula and Basmachi grades from west central Turkey. These rugs range in size from scatters up through about 7 x 10 ft. and are woven on woolen warp and weft. The pile is medium thick and wool quality is exceptional. Weaves may vary between 90 and 120 knots per square inch.

In addition there are excellent rugs in Caucasian design like Kazak, Shirvan, Baku, and other patterns being woven in Turkey today. Many of these Caucasian types from Turkey are of better quality than the limited number of rugs still woven in the Russian Caucasus and yet the Turkish rugs are less expensive because of the 45% duty still assessed against imports from the Soviet Union.

Finally, Turkey still produces a limited number of the finest handmade Orientals ever woven: Turkish silk Herekes, sometimes having 800 to 1,000 knots per square inch. These silk rugs are breathtaking in their minute detail and shimmering color (see Plate 17). There are finely woven woolen Herekes as well, rugs that resemble some of the antique Iranian Tabriz and Kashan carpets and also less expensive silk rugs like the Turkish Kayseri.

CHAPTER SIX
RUGS FROM CHINA

Throughout the 1920's there were hundreds of workshops in China weaving the thousands of rugs and carpets that came to America yearly. At that time Chinese rugs were in vogue in this country and they sold readily. The wholesale price was $1.75 to $2.25 a square foot, but only a few had worsted wool or the best Australian wool. Those that did sold for as much as $3.25 per square foot. Of course, this was an era when porterhouse steak cost $.35 a pound and a very nice home cost $10,000. The Sino-Japanese War of 1934 abruptly ended this production as looms were destroyed and any semblance of normal life in China disappeared in flames. Every year some of these rugs turn up as semi-antiques. Few seem worth the high four figure prices some dealers ask for them. Still, a good one in perfect condition is an excellent rug and a type which seems to be in fashion once again.

After World War II and through the 1950's and early 60's about the only Chinese rugs available to Americans were used, semi-antique, and antique Chinese rugs from estates and the superb Imperial and Peking rugs from Japan. These Japanese Orientals disappeared years ago, victims of Japan's inflation and re-industrialization. Some few "Chinese" rugs did come to America from Taiwan and Hong Kong, but these rugs were never important commercially. Most were purchased by tourists or by businessmen whose commitments took them to the Far East. As industry was rebuilt on the mainland after World War II the Chinese resumed rug production, but the Korean War ended any chance for trade with America during this period.

In 1976, for the first time since the early 1930's, there appeared in the New York market a good many shipments of Chinese rugs of good quality. Many importers offered these rugs on consignment to retail dealers, and in some large cities like New York department stores advertised Chinese rugs heavily. Unfortunately these rugs were all imported at the 45% duty in effect since the years of the Korean War while rugs from countries like India, Pakistan, and Iran came in at 11% duty. India had long woven excellent quality carved rugs in Chinese design that were available at one-fourth the price of the average Chinese carpet. Under the circumstances we felt the Indian carpet offered far better value--particularly because it seemed that barriers to trade with China would eventually be removed. Early in 1982 "most favored nation" trade status was extended to China and rugs were finally available at the 11% duty rate. Since then general duty rates have been reduced still further, so that at present rugs from most favored nations are assessed at a 5% duty rate, the lowest in over 60 years.

With the lowered cost and increased interest in Chinese rugs in this country, dozens of importers have rushed to purchase them. The situation is very much the same as it was in 1975 when trade was opened with Rumania. A few Rumanian rugs grew into a flood and then into a tide. Five years later importers who had been swept up in the general enthusiasm found they had to discount some of their more ill-conceived Rumanian purchases sharply in order to sell them. No doubt the same thing will happen with Chinese rugs. Those dealers who buy carefully and take the time to evaluate the market against the kinds of Chinese rugs available will do well by themselves and by their customers. Those dealers who rush headlong into the market may be disappointed.

New Chinese rugs available in today's market fall into several general groups: the two types most commonly found are the so-called "antique finish" Chinese (which resemble the carpets made and used in China before the Boxer Rebellion of 1900) and rugs in 70, 90, and 120 line quality. Antique finish Chinese are woven on unbleached cotton warp and weft, have a flexible, soft texture, and have medium to thick nap of good lustrous wool. These rugs are often slightly embossed, and colors often include a good deal of blue with ivory, coral, salmon, and gold as commonly found secondary colors. Antique finish Chinese are usually of 70 line construction: about 43 knots per square inch.

The second major group includes deeply embossed rugs with traditional designs in pastel colors. These rugs appear in different thicknesses (e.g. 3/8", 4/8", or 5/8" nap) and in different weaves. A "70 line" rug has about 43 knots per square inch, a "90 line" rug about 56 knots, and a "120 line" rug about 75 knots per square inch. Wool quality is exceptionally good, and these rugs are sturdy, heavy, and plush in feel.

Occasionally one finds offered "Chinese" rugs from Hong Kong which, although hand made, are not real Orientals at all. These rugs are hand tufted instead of knotted (the process is similar to the way in which hooked rugs are made). Appearing under a variety of trade names these rugs have four to eight tufts of large diameter wool per square inch. The strands are sealed to a foundation material with latex or a similar coating. Generally the rug has a cloth backing to cover the latex. These can be good looking rugs, but one wants to remember that the resale value will be quite low compared to that of a genuine hand knotted Oriental.

CHAPTER SEVEN
RUGS from AFGHANISTAN

Oriental rugs are woven by tribesmen of Turkoman descent in several provinces and many villages of Afghanistan in several different basic types. All of these rugs are generally classed as Afghans. We think of the traditional Afghans as having a deep rich red field with several rows of large octagonal medallions or "guls" as they are sometimes called. One of the chief characteristics of these rugs is that all still use woolen warp and weft. The wool fringe is frequently gray-brown in color. The wool used for the pile sometimes tends to be coarse in texture but is very strong and extremely hard wearing. A good Afghan rug with tight weave and thick nap is one of the most durable rugs available today.

Of course, qualities differ greatly from rug to rug. The better grade Afghans are sometimes identified as "Daulatabad" or "Mauri" rugs. Daulatabad rugs come not only in the deep maroon reds but also in lighter shades of wine. Some are available with navy fields and we have even seen pieces with medium or light green backgrounds. These new Daulatabads are very compact in weave and are actually better quality rugs than some antiques from this area (rugs called "Kiva Bokhara" by old dealers). Mauri rugs are likewise excellent in material and construction. They usually follow the old Tekke or Ersari designs from central Asia.

Another name sometimes encountered is the "Soroq." These carpets often follow the same general design as the Mauri except that the octagon medallion is more closely related to the designs of the Salor tribes than to the Tekkes. In Soroq rugs each octagon in the field is surrounded with an outer border as it was in the old Salor rugs.

Some Afghans come in light colors actually produced by a bleaching process. These rugs usually have a rosey beige or dull gold field and are sometimes called "Aqchos." We almost never buy these rugs preferring those that have not had such a heavy chemical treatment.

Besides the traditional Afghan designs we see some lovely Balouch and Beschir rugs from this weaving country. Both types use small allover patterns in a variety of colors with red and blue predominant. The Balouch rugs on the whole are quite similar to many of the Balouch coming from eastern Iran.

Most of the rugs from Afghanistan go to the wholesale markets in London and Germany. The Germans are very fond of the geometric designs and dark somber colors of these pieces. Following the invasion of Afghanistan by the Soviet Union, the availability of Afghan rugs in European and American markets actually increased as both pro-and anti-government groups sold rugs abroad to raise money for the battle back home. The long term effect of the fighting in Afghanistan can only be detrimental to rug weaving, however, as whole villages are attacked and abandoned and thousands and thousands of Afghans are forced to flee as refugees.

CHAPTER EIGHT
RUGS from RUMANIA

The real surprise in the American rug market in the mid-1970's was the sudden availability of Orientals from Rumania brought about by a decrease in U. S. customs duty. Handmade Oriental rugs have been woven in Rumania for over 200 years, ever since the Ottoman Turks occupied the Balkan countries of Europe as a part of their Ottoman Empire. Rare examples of antique Rumanian rugs are found in museums the world over. During the past fifty years we had occasionally seen Rumanian Oriental rugs in the European market. Most of these rugs went to Germany. We did not buy principally because the duty on these rugs -- from a Communist country--was 45% instead of the 11% rate then in effect for rugs from Iran, India, and Pakistan. In 1976 a new trade treaty with Rumania dropped the duty to the most favorable rate.

Hundreds of thousands of square feet of Rumanian rugs were imported into the United States in the late 1970's. They came in a rariety of qualities from average to fine in weave. The six basic qualities included:

Dorna: 26 knots per square inch
Bucharesti: 71 knots per square inch
Braila: 103 knots per square inch
Mures: 129 knots per square inch
Olt: 161 knots per square inch
Milco: 194 knots per square inch

The overwhelming majority of Rumanian rugs seen in the United States market are pieces in Bucharesti quality, but some carpets in Braila, Mures, and Olt grades also came. Even the lesser grades were good rugs, many of them comparing favorably with well known Iranian types like Tabriz, Kashan, and Isphahan. Most all these Rumanian Rugs were in traditional designs, many taken from antique rugs now in museums.

What we liked most about these Rumanian rugs was that they were naturally colored pieces without chemical treatment and yet most had exquisite soft colors and lovely sheen by reason of the excellent wool used. For the person looking for an antique at a reasonable cost the Rumanian rug was often a perfect selection, much softer in color than the rug from Iran and one-half to one-third the price of the Iranian rug in the same design.

Today the flood of Rumanian rugs coming to the United States has slowed considerably. We find ourselves selling fewer than in previous years. In large part this is because of competition from India; for the same dollars the Indian rug will be more tightly knotted than the rug from Rumania. If the two rugs are of equal weave the Indian will be less expensive. Customers continue to admire the patterns and colors of the Rumanian Orientals, but more often than not they will buy a rug from India. The future of Rumanian rugs is uncertain. Several importers have large contracts with the Rumanian government and it may be difficult for them to work off their rugs under present circumstances.

CHAPTER NINE

RUGS from RUSSIA and the CAUCASUS

Old rugs from the Caucasus (the mountainous region of southern Russia bounded by Turkey, the Black Sea, northwest Iran, and the Caspian Sea) were discovered by collectors in the early 1950's. Rug jobbers and buyers scoured the United States for these rural and village rugs with their bold geometric designs and strong primary colors. Values shot up with thousands of choice antique Caucasians exported from America to Germany and elsewhere. There is less activity nowadays as fewer German buyers come to America. Still, jobbers and antique dealers continue to look for old Caucasians, sometimes paying very high prices in hopes of selling these pieces, even worn and thin rugs, at a good profit abroad. Certainly an antique Caucasian of excellent quality in good condition is a valuable rug, but few old Caucasians now available are so choice. Big prices are asked of, and paid by, uninformed customers for worn out, inferior rugs.

Most of the Caucasians which bring such high prices are rugs woven in the 19th century (there is some debate over just how old some of these pieces are or where exactly they were woven). The situation is complicated by the fact that after the Revolution of 1917 the Russian government commercialized rug weaving in the Caucasus as a way of earning foreign exchange. There were "five year plan" rugs produced in the 1920's and 1930's intended principally for export. For the most part these rugs are not nearly as interesting nor as valuable as the Caucasian weavings of the earlier period, but they can be confused with the earlier types by an inexperienced buyer.

There are still "real" Caucasian rugs woven in southern Russia but these modern rugs are assessed a 45% import duty if brought to the United States (compared with 5% duty on rugs from most other weaving areas). The artificially high cost of contemporary Russian rugs means their market is limited and leads us to recommend in their place rugs in geometric design from Turkey, from Pakistan, from India, and elsewhere. The excellent village rugs from Turkey often employ Caucasian designs as do the Shirvan rugs from the Jaipur area of northern India and the fine Kafkazi rugs from Pakistan. An Indian or Pakistani rug in Caucasian design is almost always finely woven—many have 145 knots per square inch. Wages are not high in these countries and so their rugs represent good value.

The hobbyist or collector will prefer the old Caucasian but he must be prepared to pay the price for his decision. The old Caucasian will be expensive in dollars and may well be thin or delicate in condition and so unsuitable for use on the floor except in a very protected location. Remember that the rug dealer's "antique" is sometimes nothing more than a mediocre old rug. A choice antique should be a piece unusual enough to merit special status and should be a rug in good condition.

In addition to the Caucasus, modern day Russia includes the area of Russian Turkestan which produced the fine "Bokharas" of old ("Bokhara" is the name of a city in Turkestan which was applied to Turkoman rugs by some dealers in the 19th century). In that section of Russia where Turkoman tribes once herded sheep, some styles of Bokhara rugs are still woven. Most new Turkomans from Russia appear in Tekke or Youmud design, and some are fine in weave and closely clipped. Some of these better quality Turkoman rugs resemble the fine quality geometric types woven in Pakistan for the European trade. These Russian Bokharas are expensive because of the unfavorable duty rate assessed against them. They are not of much importance in today's market.

CHAPTER TEN
RUGS from OTHER WEAVING AREAS

RUGS from JAPAN

After World War II Japan produced several types of hand woven Oriental rugs for export. Among them was a very superior rug on the order of a Chinese or Savonnerie design under the trade name of Imperial. These rugs -- thick and heavy, with excellent quality wool and carved nap--sold for about $5.00 per square foot in the mid-1950's. Unfortunately prices rose rapidly as Japan industrialized. By about 1965 the Imperial had become so expensive that there was very little interest in them in this country.

Another rug, the Peking, was the last to go from the market. It was not quite as fine as the Imperial and so remained a bit less expensive longer. Another type of Oriental imported from Japan was the Fuigi Royal. It also was excellent in workmanship and materials but disappeared from the market even before the Imperial.

Hand knotted rugs are still woven on a very limited scale in Japan, but virtually none are exported. We have not seen significant numbers of Orientals from Japan in the various wholesale markets for well over a decade. This account is given and these names mentioned to help the reader who may find one of these rugs offered at an estate or house sale.

RUGS from EGYPT

It may surprise you to learn that Oriental rugs are woven in Egypt today. We were surprised in 1975 to see a million dollars or more of hand woven rugs in Persian designs from Egypt in a London warehouse. Practically all were in 7 x 10 ft. or 9 x 12 ft. sizes and all were a feeble attempt at a Kashan design. We have known that some rugs have always been woven in Egypt but never have they appeared in numbers in commercial channels. The fact is that these rugs were woven to repay Russia for the arms and weapons it provided to Egypt. Russia sent these Egyptian Kashans to the bonded warehouses in London hoping to find buyers for them.

These rugs attempted to copy Kashans like the one shown in Plate 3. Most had more blue than red. The weave was not good and they did not appear to be very desirable when all factors were considered. Actually they lacked the body, the weave, and the beauty of better quality Kashans. Recently there have appeared handmade Egyptian rugs in Tabriz design as well. These usually have central medallion designs with typical Tabriz colors of rust, gold, green, and ivory. Once again we have not been impressed by the workmanship and finishing of most Egyptian rugs we have seen to date. If color, design, and quality continue to improve Egyptian rugs might begin to threaten the sales of rugs from the Balkans, but that day is far off at present.

RUGS from SPAIN

We know there has been considerable weaving of rugs in Spain. They have generally been handled by some one or two importers specializing in this type. Still, they are not a real factor in the American market. I know that some individuals, visiting or wintering in Spain, may buy a rug or two. The rugs they bring back tend to be rather loosely woven of fair to good wool. Designs are frequently all over patterns reminiscent of the familiar Herati motif found in some Persian rugs.

RUGS from FRANCE

There have been no rugs imported commercially from France in over fifty years. Very few have been made since before World War I. These rugs, all antiques by now, were in the form of the thin tapestry weave Aubusson type or the thick, pile weave Savonnerie rugs. Both types were in the same general designs: formal, floral, rococco patterns with elaborate medallions, corner pieces, and floral borders. Those that we bought during the 1930's were usually woven in Austria or Rumania. They were very like the old French Savonnneries in design and construction.

RUGS from GREECE

There are a limited number of hand woven rugs made in Greece, but most are for the domestic market. Only on occasion does a tourist buy one or two. Certainly the great flood of Greek Spartas that came to America between World War I and II has ceased completely. For the most part these rugs were garish, cheap, and very poorly made. They have not been missed.

RUGS from YUGOSLAVIA

A few rugs about 9 x 12 ft. in Persian designs have appeared in the markets over the years. Most importers would not make a second purchase as they did not find ready buyers among retail dealers. Today I do not think these rugs would have a chance to compete with the excellent Rumanian production.

RUGS from BULGARIA

Although introduced to rug weaving in the same way as were the Rumanians, the Bulgarians have been less fortunate politically. They weave some Persian design rugs in good qualities but these rugs land in the United States under 45% duty. They simply cannot compete with the values available from Rumania.

RUGS from NEPAL

We have seen a few rugs in the wholesale markets woven by Tibetan refugees displaced into Nepal when China annexed their country in the 1960's. Some of these rugs come through India and in fact some Tibetan rugs are woven in India. Most all rugs of this type appear in designs characteristic of China or Chinese Turkestan. Most are loosely woven, not nearly as dense as a new Chinese rug.

Some Tibetan rugs have simple floral or geometric designs woven in one color on a contrasting background. Wool quality can be quite good, but the appeal of these rugs is definitely limited.

RUGS from MOROCCO

Morocco has been producing weavings for some time, mostly for sale to the tourists who visit the area. Technical characteristics can vary greatly from the piled rugs found in most other weaving areas, and in fact many of the Moroccan rugs are flat weaves in simple geometric designs. Many rugs are very coarse and use materials other than cotton, wool, silk, or the like. The foundation (and sometimes even the pile) of these rugs is often made of jute or sisal. Sometimes the pile is a blend of wool and jute. Designs tend to be geometric and colors earthtones of brown, black, and cream. These rugs are very cheap and are not very durable.

PART II

ALPHABETICAL LISTING and DESCRIPTION OF TYPES

The purpose of this book, and especially this section, is to give the most up-to-date information possible on the changes affecting the types of rugs listed in Colonel Jacobsen's ORIENTAL RUGS - A COMPLETE GUIDE (published in 1962) and more especially to give details on the many new types being woven in India, Pakistan, Rumania, Turkey, China, Afghanistan, and Russia.

Of course, there have been wholesale changes in the availability of some rug types in the past decade--even the virtual disappearance from the markets of many famous types of rugs. In the place of many of the types from Iran today's customer will find rugs from India, Pakistan, China, and elsewhere. The alphabetical list of rugs that follows cannot hope to be an absolutely complete list of all types. Many of the Iranian types are listed, but the intention is more to describe the types a rug buyer would find in a dealer's shop than the rug varieties he would see in a museum or specialist's collection. When you consider that Pakistan is making many rugs in various Iranian designs, that India is turning almost entirely to weaving such types, and that Rumania and Turkey are also producing many kinds of rugs not seen in the markets for many years, one realizes the difficulty of providing useful information about every single kind of Oriental rug now available.

We have listed rugs from India under the appropriate rug type. Do not be surprised to find some dealers using individual names like "Agra" or "Laristan" for Indian types. You will find rugs of similar design listed together under one heading regardless of country of origin (for instance the heading "Kashan" discusses rugs of this type from Iran, India, Pakistan, and Rumania). In talking about a specific rug with a customer, all reputable dealers will be quick to identify the origin of the rug: "a fine Pakistani Kashan," or "a Sarouk from India," or "a Bucharesti grade Tabriz from Rumania" are all typical identifications. Some dealers may use less specific names ("Agra" and "Balkan" are examples), or even wholly invented names that are not known to others. As always it is most comforting to do business with someone who knows his stock thoroughly and can give accurate information about the carpet.

ABADEH

FROM IRAN - This is a name that does not appear in Colonel Jacobsen's COMPLETE GUIDE. The type began to appear in quantity in the late 1960's; better quality Abadehs were among the best woven rugs available from Iran during this period. All were woven on cotton warp and weft and most were tightly woven with rather closely clipped to medium thick nap. Because the nap was often closely trimmed by the weaver, the design of the rug was usually sharp and crisp. However, a poor quality Abadeh from Iran is a mediocre rug by any meaure; lumpy weave, muddy colors, and bad wool are all problems that sometimes appeared.

Abadeh rugs are almost always in the same general design as Plate 14; usually a clear red field with small geometric medallion and matching corners, stylized tree of life design at either end, and tiny jewel-like geometric figures filling the field. Woven in the Fars district of southern Iran, Abadeh rugs somewhat resemble Shiraz in their geometric design, but Abadehs are usually more tightly knotted. Some Abadehs come with tan or medium blue background and a few occasionally are found with an allover floral design filling the field. Sizes range from 2 x 3 ft. through 2½ x 4 ft., 2 x 5 ft., 3½ x 5 ft., 7 x 5 ft., and through 7 x 10 ft. A few runners about 3 x 8 to 10 ft. came, as did an occasional square rug of 6 x 6 ft. or 8 x 8 ft. There were no 8 x 10 ft. or larger sizes because there were not large looms in the area.

FROM INDIA - Abadeh rugs are available in many sizes and several qualities from India, most all resembling the rug in Plate 14 in color and design. Sizes range from 2 x 3 ft. mats through carpets larger than 10 x 14 ft. Abadeh rugs from India are often thicker than their Iranian counterparts.

FROM RUMANIA - Occasionally Rumanian rugs are found in Abadeh designs, but these rugs more often have rust, brick red, navy, or ivory backgrounds in place of the true red of the Iranian or India types (see Plate 24). Rumanian Abadehs come in sizes up through 10 x 14 ft., and sometimes larger still.

AFGHAN RUGS
From Afghanistan

The typical Afghan has some shade of red or wine red field with rows of small octagonal medallions or "guls" filling the central ground (see Plate 23). Often the octagons will be quartered in midnight blue (almost black) and ivory or tan. Sometimes gold, orange, rust, or green appears as an accent color. Afghans today remain of all wool construction--even the warp and weft of the rug is usually a natural brown or greyish-brown wool. A typical Afghan is a thick and compact rug, although most are not finely woven. Because of the excellent wool used and very stout construction, most average to better grade Afghans will be very durable. Afghans come in small sizes ("Poshtis") of less than 2 x 3 ft. up through carpet and runner dimensions. There can be considerable variety in quality as well with a typical better grade "Daultabad" Afghan more tightly knotted but with more closely clipped construction than the average quality rug. In the 2½ x 4 ft. and 3 x 5 ft. sizes Afghans often come in prayer designs, sometimes with buff or navy blue grounds.

It is difficult to predict what the future will hold for rugs from Afghanistan. Good numbers of Afghans have been available in the recent past, but the continuing fighting in the countryside and virtual exile of hundreds of thousands of villagers must eventually slow rug production. If Afghanistan falls completely within the sphere of Soviet Russia, U. S. customs duty may be raised to the 45% rate which would further discourage Afghan imports. An age-old culture is ending today for millions of Afghans, and similar happenings in the past in other rug weaving countries leads one to expect fewer and less interesting rugs in the future.

AFSHAR RUGS

FROM IRAN - Most Afshars come from southern Iran, and there are two general types found, the "regular" Afshar woven in the countryside or in small villages and the more tightly knotted and generally superior "Kirman Afshar." Most all Afshar rugs are geometric in design (see Plate 39) and most have strong reds and blues as primary colors with accents of gold, rust, bright green, and a nearly purple blue. Most all village Afshars are woven on woolen warp and weft but some more tightly woven Kirman Afshars come on cotton foundation. The wool pile sometimes feels dry and cotton-like. Few Afshars appear in sizes larger than about 7 x 5 ft., and scatter rugs in nearly square proportion are not unusual. Present prices are too high to be competitive with rugs of similar quality from other countries.

FROM INDIA - Some rugs in Afshar patterns have been made in India for both the German market (where they are quite popular) and for America. The wool of these Indian Afshars is often better than that of the Iranians, and there is more variety in dimensions available. Often the Indian Afshar is a thicker and heavier rug, and it is invariably woven on a cotton warp and weft.

AGRA RUGS
From India

Never available in sizes smaller than about 9 x 12 ft., one does not even find an old one from an estate any more. With open ground, floral medallion and borders, and soft olive green, fawn, tan, and blue colors, Agra rugs were formal in style and muted in appearance. Do not be surprised to find this name resurrected by someone for new rugs sooner or later. For more information about the old style Agras, see the entry in the COMPLETE GUIDE, pg. 167.

AHAR RUGS
From Iran

A member of the Herez family, but slightly different from the typical Herez in that these rugs often have a more curvilinear than geometric design. Excellent quality, one of the best of the Herez, heavy and compact with good wool. Very few available. New ones cost more than a semi-antique that might be bought from a private home, even though the semi-old one should be more valuable. Most are in carpet sizes. Some small sizes in new rugs approximately 2½ x 3½ and 3½ x 5 ft. Scarce and expensive.

The pattern usually consists of a large central medallion and corners to match. Rusty red, navy, medium blue, and a good bit of ivory are common. Not finely woven in comparison to some other Persian types, but very durable and hard wearing.

We have seen few Ahars in the market in the past several years. As the price of average quality Iranian Herez rugs increased, Ahars grew more expensive still, making them less and less competitive with Herez rugs from India and Rumania.

ANATOLIAN RUGS
From Turkey

Any Turkish rug can be called "Anatolian" as the names are synonymous. We used to refer to all the old Turkish mats as "Anatolians" and some museums still refer to rare Turkish rugs as Anatolians. It is sometimes difficult to say exactly where a rug comes from in Turkey, especially if it is a very old piece . . . hence the general name "Anatolian" as a generic type (in the same way "Persian" can be used for all those rugs from Iran).

ANIMAL CARPETS
From Iran, India, Rumania, and Pakistan

There were not many new animal rugs available before the mid-1960's. Most of the rugs with figural designs that did appear were old rugs. With the advent of the Taba-Tabaie Tabriz, the use of the classic animal designs increased greatly. Approximately one out of four of these new Tabriz came with the animal or hunting design. There is little difference between these two patterns. Both are old 16th century designs reinterpreted by modern weavers. Of course, some animal rugs are more beautiful than others. It is important not to have the animals or hunters too large or too conspicuous (see "Tabriz" and "Taba-Tabaie Tabriz").

The Qum rugs ("Ghoum" and "Ghum" are alternate spellings) employ animal designs quite frequently--both in rugs with woolen nap and with silk pile. Most animal design Qums are in small sizes up to 5 x 8 ft., but there are some few as large as 7 x 10 and even 9 x 12 ft. sizes appear.

We find many animal carpets and hunting carpets in several qualities among the rugs from India and Rumania. Some of these are strikingly beautiful designs. Most of the patterns are taken from famous old animal carpets in different museums. The Rumanians do a wonderful job of interpreting these designs in very fine rugs and also in good average rugs (see Plates 5 and 52).

We have seen a few animal design rugs from Pakistan in fine weaves. These are mostly Pakistani versions of Kashan and Tabriz patterns, and have been available so far primarily in scatter sizes.

ARAK RUGS
From Iran

Rugs in medium and large carpet size, and in floral designs woven in the vicinity of the city of Arak in central Iran, Arak rugs were plentiful and popular in the years before World War II and just after. No new Araks from Iran have been available. Remember that the city of Arak and its vicinity is where most Sarouks were made. Sarouk too is expensive today. Arak was a lesser quality rug than the Sarouk and generally different from Sarouk in that it used only the more traditional floral designs. Araks were good rugs, thicker and heavier than Sultanabads and far superior to the Mahal or Muskabad. It was often hard to draw the line of demarcation between the Arak and the Mahal or the Sultanabad. The Muskabad was always cheaper and brighter---the coarsest of the group.

Few customers will pay the big price asked for the lower grade Mahals and Muskabads today when good, floral design rugs are available from India at a fraction of the price. The Indian carpet will not only be less expensive than the Arak, but probably more finely knotted as well. An occasional Arak may be found at an estate sale, and if in good condition would be a good value at the right price.

ARDEBIL RUGS
From Iran

Rugs of this type come from the vicinity of the city of Ardebil in extreme northwestern Iran, near the border of Soviet Azerbaijan and the Caucasus Mountains. As might be expected, Ardebils share the strong geometric designs and primary colors of the Caucasian types. Unlike most Caucasians, almost all Ardebils are woven on cotton warp and weft. Most have average to medium fine weave with medium thick pile. Ardebils often have soft ivory, green, or rust backgrounds, sometimes with angular pole medallion designs and sometimes with geometric allover patterns (see Plate 36). Many, many Ardebils came in a large dozer size, about 7 x 4½ ft., but small mats through 10 x 14 ft. and 12 x 15 ft. carpets also appeared, as did medium length runners.

In the 1960's and early 1970's Ardebil rugs were popular and fairly cheap. Old Caucasian rugs were already expensive and Ardebils sold to many buyers who preferred the Caucasian look but wanted less costly rugs. By the 1970's the quality of many new Ardebil rugs had declined significantly and prices were very high. Most buyers preferred the fine geometrics from Pakistan and Jaipur in northern India which were better made and one-half the price.

Ardebil rugs as a type should not be confused with the most famous Oriental rug in the world, the Ardebil Mosque carpet in the Victoria and Albert Museum in London. This huge, finely woven carpet measures 34 ft. x 17 ft. and was purchased in Ardebil by representatives of a British carpet firm in the 1880's. An inscription dates the carpet to the year 1539, but it is all but certain that the carpet was not woven in Ardebil. Over the years the cities of Kashan, Tabriz, and even Isphahan have been suggested as the place of origin of this magnificent rug. Rugs in the same pattern are often called Ardebil Mosque designs.

AUBUSSON RUGS

FROM FRANCE - These tapestry-technique, non-piled carpets have not been woven in France since before World War I. Even the few old ones that came from Russia in the 1930's seldom reappear in the market these days, and few come from estates. This is a type appropriate for certain 18th century restorations, as the type was available and in vogue when European settlers built at Williamsburg and other colonial centers.

FROM INDIA - There are sometimes available new flat weave Aubusson-style rugs from India. "Jewel of Kashmir" rugs were inexpensive in the early 1960's but increased in cost until they were nearly as costly as piled Savonnerie rugs of the same size. Because the flat weave construction is not nearly as durable as a napped rug, most buyers have preferred the Savonnerie style.

BAHKTIARI RUGS
From Iran

This type can be divided into two general categories: the excellent quality wool foundation rugs in scatter sizes found in the markets in the 1920's and 30's and the rugs and carpets on (mostly) cotton warp and weft which came after World War II and which were more commercial in character. Few nomadic types were superior to the bag faces and dozar-sized (about 6½ x 4½ ft.) scatters of the first category. The wool quality in particular was outstanding, and even a few years' use often developed that lovely patina and sheen for which such rugs were so prized. Patterns were strong geometric designs with angular stars, rosettes, and other angular figures. After World War II carpets appeared bearing the Bahktiari name, but these were in some ways less interesting and less varied. In larger sizes (10 x 12 and 10 x 14 ft.) these Bahktiaris often had garden designs, wherein the central field was divided into rows of rectangles with repeated blossom, flower, or prayer arch designs. Colors were usually medium brown, gold, navies, and greens.

As Western ways came to the more primitive areas of Iran in the 1960's the production of carpets gave way to light manufacturing, and costs rose sharply. A good semi-antique Bahktiari might be found from an estate, but few buyers would consider a new rug of this type at the price which would have to be asked for it.

BAKSHIS RUGS
From Iran

The famous old rugs by this name were very like the old Feraghans with all-over stylized floral design and supple weave. Rugs of this type were rare 60 years ago, and when found were often worn thin. Today the name is associated with a variety of Herez rug, usually a rug more curvilinear in design than the typical Herez. Most all rugs of this type would be imported as Herez, although occasionally one finds a Bakshis listed on a bill of lading. Bakshis and Ahar are the two best types coming from the Herez district today, but as with Ahar Bakshis rugs are so expensive as to make most buyers look to less costly types from India or Rumania.

BAKU RUGS
From the Caucasus

Old Baku rugs (from the city of this name on the west shore of the Caspian Sea) are not a factor in today's market. Even though Colonel Jacobsen discussed these rugs in his COMPLETE GUIDE they were always in very short supply. A Baku is one of the rarest of all the Caucasian types and seldom found even in collectors' estates (Good hunting!).

There have appeared a few new Bakus true in color and design to the classic old rugs in the London market in past years but the city of Baku is in the Soviet Union, and so these rugs would land in the United States at the 45% duty rate. Some of the rugs from Turkey in Caucasian motif resemble the colors and pattern of old Baku rugs, and one of these pieces would be a much better value in today's market.

BALKAN RUGS

Sometimes used as a generic identification for any Oriental from Rumania, Yugoslavia, Bulgaria, or Albania. It is important that the exact country of origin be known if you are considering a new rug from one of these countries since at present only Rumanian rugs land under the preferential most-favored nation duty rate. The 40% difference in U. S. customs duty between imports from Rumania and the other Balkan countries can make a big difference in the price of the rug.

BALUCHI RUGS

(Also called "Belouch," "Belooch," "Baluchistan" rugs)

From Iran and Afghanistan

In years past there were not large numbers of these more primitive, tribal rugs available in America. With their very dark and somber colors of red, indigo, black, and browns and strong geometric patterns they seemed to appeal more to European buyers than to Americans (see Plate 22). Rug dealers of Iranian descent sometimes seemed prejudiced against these rugs, preferring to sell types like Shiraz or Yalameh instead of rugs woven by Baluchis.

In the late 1960's there developed considerable interest in tribal weavings including utilitarian pieces like carrying bags, bedding bags, animal trappings, and the like, and the Baluchi tribes in Iran and especially in Afghanistan supplied many such objects. Baluchi rugs were seen from a different perspective--as one of the less commercial types still available--and the scatter sized area rugs and prayer rugs available in the recent past have found ready buyers.

Baluchi rugs still come more often than not on woolen warp and weft, but some fine Baluchi rugs from Iran sometimes have a warp of cotton or of wool and cotton blend. Iranian Baluchi rugs are often more colorful than Afghan Baluchi, with rich red grounds or borders and with accents of bright green, orange, medium blue, and chrome yellow. Afghan Baluchi rugs are sometimes so subdued in color that bright light is needed to pick out the black design against indigo background. As might be expected, Baluchi rugs from Iran can cost several times as much as Baluchis from Afghanistan of the same quality. Sizes are limited to smaller dimensions because the rugs are woven on primitive horizontal ground looms: principally 2½ x 4 ft. through about 7 x 4 ft., with very few available even as large as 5 x 9 ft.

BERGAMO RUGS

From Turkey

Pre-World War I Bergamos still rank as one of the choicest of collector's rugs. Unfortunately they are seldom available today even from estates and like other antiques would be expensive if in even average condition. Old Bergamos--like so many other types of antique rugs--are not really a factor in today's market.

The good news is that Bergamo rugs are available again from Turkey for the first time in 60 years. Such rugs were not available in the market until the 1970's. We stopped visiting Turkey to seek rugs many years ago since it had become so impossible to find presentable rugs. Now there are fairly good numbers of good quality Turkish rugs in the markets. Still, not all by any means have the designs and colors of the old Bergamos, Melez, Ghiordes, and other great Turkish types. As always rugs must be carefully selected with color, pattern, materials, and weave all evaluated before the rug is chosen. The new rugs we do find in old patterns are lovely indeed.

Our advice is not to look for an old Bergamo . . . but you can inquire for one of the better new ones. Most all are in scatter sizes up to 5 x 8 ft. and most have good weave of about 100 knots per square inch, medium thick nap, and warp and weft of wool.

BESCHIR RUGS
From Russia and Afghanistan

Similar in texture and feel to heavy Daulatabad Afghans, we see few Beschir rugs in America. They are quite popular in Europe, even though good ones are expensive. Occasionally a Beschir appears with a medallion design, but more frequently they use an allover pattern of stylized blossoms or other floral elements. Border designs often resemble the patterns used in some Afghans. These rugs are hard wearing and durable. Available in limited numbers in small scatter sizes and carpets often with rich midnight blue background and red borders. Not a type you will find in most rug stores in America.

BIBIKABAD RUGS
From Iran

Fifteen years ago Bibikabads were in abundance in sizes from 3½ x 5 ft. to 7 x 4½ ft., and especially in 9 x 12 ft. and large carpet sizes. Some also came in intermediate sizes such as 6 x 9 and 8 x 10 ft. Today very few new ones are found and when available these new rugs are about three times the price of ten years ago, too high to be readily saleable. Bibikabad is a rug from the Hamadan weaving district in Iran and high labor costs caused most Hamadans to increase sharply in price in the late 1960's.

In addition, the quality of new Bibikabads seems to have deteriorated. Unless prices moderate considerably, the only ones we would recommend would be used rugs taken in trade or purchased from estates. Most of these older rugs will be in good condition and better in quality than the new ones. We find we can frequently sell used and semi-antique Bibikabads at retail for less than current wholesale prices. We do not offer them at all unless we can sell them for less than market prices in New York.

BIJAR RUGS

FROM IRAN - Bijar rugs from Iran are limited in supply in today's market. In the past fifteen years Iranian rugs of this type have increased in cost by three to four hundred percent. Since World War II Bijars have been available mostly in scatter sizes (4 x 2½, 3½ x 5, 7 x 4 ft.) although the supply of carpets increased substantially in the late 1970's. Many of those made after World War II were more finely woven than the Bijars made before that time. Many had red and tomato red fields and the allover Herati design was often used. These rugs were frequently irregular in shape--more so than any other type of Persian rug. In the late 1970's there began to appear extremely fine Bijars with weaves of 300 or more knots per square inch. These new fine Bijars are almost always on cotton warp and weft. Nap is thick and the rugs extremely heavy and compact.

Among the most beautiful and valuable of the Bijars were the coarser antique Bijars made prior to World War I by Kurdish tribesman before they settled in and around the city of Bijar. These rugs came in a variety of both geometric and floral designs, and were some of the most admired rugs by collectors in spite of their coarseness. Most all of these older Bijars were woven on woolen warp and weft. Today very few of these old Bijars appear even from estates.

FROM INDIA - There are some excellent Bijars from India available today.

With weaves of 200 knots per square inch or so and excellent wool, many of these pieces have the classic Herati field design with angular medallions and corner brackets (see Plate 10). Colors are most often rich reds and blues with accents of turquoise, gold, salmon, and green.

BIRJAND RUGS
From Iran

This name refers to the lowest quality of rugs from the Khurasan District and the city of Meshed. They once came to America in great numbers in carpet sizes, but few if any have come to the American market in fifteen years. Evidently many of these rugs were sold in the Iranian domestic market in the 1960's. The old ones were beautiful and did last 25 years or more in spite of their relative coarseness.

BOKHARA RUGS

A beginner can easily be confused by the name Bokhara. There are rugs available today by this name from Iran, Russia, Afghanistan, Pakistan, and India. Originally the only "Bokhara" rugs were the product of the nomadic Turkoman tribesmen roaming the area east of the Caspian Sea and north of Iran. Most of these rugs passed into commercial channels through the city of Bokhara located in what is now Russian Turkestan, and it was the name of this market city that was given as a general name to this kind of rug. As Russia grew into a world power at the end of the 19th century, the relationship between the nomadic Turkoman and the Czarist bureaucrats became more and more uneasy. It soon became the policy of the Russian government to forcibly subdue the wandering Turkoman peoples. The Turkoman owed no allegiance except to their own tribes, and thus were regarded as a threat to the government in Moscow. A military campaign to subdue the Turkoman was begun and the result was the end of a way of life for these nomads, and a drastic reduction in the number of Turkoman "Bokharas" available.

Fortunately, not all weaving ended. Some Turkoman tribes continued to wander northern Iran and others followed their age old ways in Afghanistan. Eventually, the Bokhara patterns made their way to Pakistan, and finally to India. Thus today there are antique "Bokhara" rugs from Russian Turkestan, along with newer Bokhara rugs from Iran, Afghanistan, Pakistan, and India.

FROM RUSSIA - Old Bokharas from Russian Turkestan are seldom available in today's market. Occasionally one appears from an estate in this country but there are few antique rugs left in Russia today. The Russians gathered many together and exported them by the hundreds in the 1930's as a way of earning foreign exchange. We bought many rare and choice Tekke, Pinde, Salor, and Yomud Bokharas in the London market at that time. Since World War II we have imported none, nor have we seen many in the New York market. Some Russian Bokharas are still seen at times in the London warehouses, but most are offered by lot only. You cannot buy anything less than the whole lot, and out of the group of fifty or one hundred rugs, perhaps only five are desirable pieces. If the import duty on Russian goods is reduced to 5% instead of 45% there is the possibility that some of these Bokharas will appear in America. In the meantime the only possibility of a choice old rug is from an estate.

FROM IRAN - The Turkoman of northern Iran (mostly Yomud tribesmen) have produced in the past and continue to weave today Bokhara rugs of several types. Most of these rugs are in old Tekke designs and colors, although some are in characteristically Yomud patterns. Up until the great surge in production from Pakistan these Iranian Bokharas were available in America at very reasonable prices. Today very few Bokharas from Iran come to America. They have been driven from the market by the lovely but much less expensive Bokharas from Pakistan. The Persian Bokhara is a very good rug, stoutly made of good wool and very durable, but it cannot compete with the much less expensive rugs in similar design from Pakistan.

FROM AFGHANISTAN - Few fine Bokharas from Afghanistan are seen in America although such rugs are woven. We are much more familiar with the thicker less tightly woven Afghans. Most Afghan Bokharas go to Europe, to Switzerland and to Germany. They closely resemble Pakistani Bokharas in pattern and colors, with the exception that most continue to be woven on woolen foundation.

FROM PAKISTAN - In the last twenty or twenty-five years the word Bokhara has meant rugs from Pakistan as far as we in America are concerned. In the 1950's the weaving of many different qualities of rugs in the old Bokhara pattern became commercially important in Pakistan. The carpet industry has by now become very large and an important source of foreign currency for the country. Most of these Pakistani rugs are in Tekke or, much less frequently, Yomud designs. All are woven on a cotton foundation. Quality ranges from coarsely woven, inexpensive utility rugs to very fine and choice pieces. A good Karachi grade Bokhara is one of the thickest, loveliest rugs available today. The Pakistani government subsidized the carpet industry until the late 1960's, making these rugs an even better bargain during those years. The subsidies have been ended now but even so Bokhara rugs have not risen in cost nearly as much as have the majority of Iranian types.

The first Pakistani Bokharas coming to this country were almost invariably in a Tekke pattern with some shade of wine red as the field color (see Plate 16). In the last decade the variety of colors has been expanded dramatically and a wider choice of designs is also available. We are beginning, in fact, to see new designs appear that are the inventions of the Pakistani weavers themselves. Some of these new geometric pieces do not look much like old Turkoman Bokharas, but many are handsome rugs in their own right.

For more information, see the chapter on "Rugs from Pakistan" in Part I.

BORCHALOU RUGS
From Iran

Ten to fifteen years ago rugs of this type from the Hamadan area in Iran were rather plentiful in two sizes–3½ x 5 and 5 x 7 ft. There were a few short runners and a few rugs as large as 5 x 10 ft. Borchalous often had more curvilinear and floral designs than other varieties of Hamadan rugs and they were better in quality than most average Hamadans. Thirty and forty year old Borchalous were available in great numbers up until about 1970 in the London market; most were about 5 x 7 ft. in size. Since then availability has declined drastically and prices have risen by nearly 300%.

New Borchalous were often bright in color, but many of the pieces sold as new in the late 1950's and early 1960's will have begun to soften in color. These are good substantial rugs. Most are rather floral in design although there are frequently strong geometric elements present. Borchalous will not be missed too much as there are other new rugs we like better like some of the excellent Indian Sarouks. A semi-antique Borchalou in good condition and with a good weave will give very excellent service.

"BRAILA" QUALITY RUGS
From Rumania

This name indicates a quality and not a type of rug. This is one of the better grades from Rumania and is a very excellent rug, all handmade, 100% wood nap with about 103 knots to the square inch (most all Rumanian rugs have a tag affixed to the back specifying the quality). The Braila grade appears in many Persian designs like Tabriz, Kashan, Qum, Isphahan, and Sarouk. Rugs in Braila quality are available in sizes from small scatters to carpet sizes as large as 17 x 13 ft. Rumanian rugs are likely to be tagged as "Tabriz from Rumania," or perhaps "Braila grade rug from Rumania in Tabriz design" or "Sarouk design," etc. Turn to "Rumanian Rugs" in Part I for details.

"BUCHARESTI" QUALITY RUGS
From Rumania

This name indicates one of the several different rug qualities woven in Rumania today. A Bucharesti grade rug is medium in quality, having about 70 Senna knots to the square inch (which makes them more compact than all the Iranian Muskabads, Mahals, and Sultanabads, and most of the Araks and Herez.) These rugs use an excellent grade of carpet wool and have proven to be durable.

We have seen a variety of patterns among Bucharesti quality rugs from Rumania. Tabriz designs are the most common but Sarouk, Qum, Isphahan, Kashan, and even some geometrics are found. One feature of most all the Bucharesti quality rugs are the soft, lovely colors employed. The tones are frequently as subtle as those in a choice new Persian Tabriz. One simply cannot buy a Persian Tabriz in today's market that compares with the Rumanian rug for the price. A rug from Iran costing the same as a Bucharesti Rumanian is neither as good nor as beautiful a carpet.

CHAUDOR RUGS
From Russia and Afghanistan

No new Turkoman Chaudor rugs or bags have been available for over a generation. Often considered a subtribe of the Youmuds, the Chaudor wove thick, heavy carpets and utilitarian pieces. Tent bags and bag faces are still sometimes available from estates.

CHI-CHI RUGS
From the Caucasus

One of the rarest and most sought after of Caucasian types, the old Chi-Chi rugs available in the U. S. and in the European market have all been bought from American dealers who got them from estates and individuals in this country. No semi-old Chi-Chi rugs have been imported to America since the 1930's. They are one of the highest priced of the Caucasian types. Most are in sizes of 3 x 5 and 4 x 6 ft. So few come on the market that one might be willing to pay almost any price for a good antique Chi-Chi and still search in vain for years to find one.

Suprisingly we have seen no new Chi-Chi rugs among the new Russian rugs we have examined. New Kabistan, Shirvan, Daghestan, Kazak, and even Baku have appeared but no Chi-Chi. Some rugs in this design may still be woven in Russia but we have yet to happen upon any. Occasionally one does find a Turkish village rug with Chi-Chi design, and a rug like this can represent an excellent combination of value and practicality.

CHINESE RUGS

Very few of the Chinese rugs of the period from 1920 to 1935 are in good condition today. These rugs are often a bit thin, as can be seen from the presence of white knots in the field (these are knots in the warp strings originally hidden by the thick nap). Even if the nap is thick such rugs often have bad shadings or spots that hurt their value.

New Chinese rugs have been imported in great numbers in the past several years in the qualities described in Chapter Six. There is competition among various dealers, and so it pays to shop carefully. Although most new Chinese rugs continue to appear in the soft pastels and floral designs of years past, we have seen some Chinese in Iranian Tabriz, Kashan, and Kirman designs.

DAGHESTAN RUGS
From the Caucasus

No old Daghestan rugs have been imported to this country since about 1938. Those rugs were old ones confiscated by the Russian government and turned into cash in London and New York. As noted in Colonel Jacobsen's COMPLETE GUIDE, the Germans have bought all the Daghestans, both excellent and poor, that they could find in America. They have pushed the prices of these rugs up beyond reason.

Most old ones are worn and not too valuable while a choice one in good condition is worth a very substantial amount. Very few appear and only one out of

100 fits the category of being choice and in good condition.

As a label "Daghestan" includes rugs of somewhat varied construction, but most dealers would agree on certain design features. In many cases Daghestans have an all-over lattice-like design consisting of repeated small angular palmettes or blossoms, often on a gold, ivory, or navy blue field (see Plate 40). To the hand Daghestans are usually rather more tightly knotted than Caucasian types like Kazak, and usually have fairly thin nap, even if in good condition. Prayer patterns are common.

Occasionally rugs with Daghestan motif are found in Turkey. With good wool and compact weave, these Turkish rugs are wonderful values, rugs which can be used under any conditions of traffic.

DERBEND RUGS
From the Caucasus

Derbend is a port city on the Caspian Sea; it is likely that the name of the city became transferred to some of the rug types which were marketed there. Rugs identified as Derbend seem often more thickly napped and perhaps not as tightly woven as Daghestan, Kuba, or some other Caucasian types. No new Derbends are available.

DERGAZINE RUGS
From Iran

In the 1960's there were literally thousands of Dergazine rugs and runners available from the Hamadan weaving district of Iran. Each importing house had stocks of 2 x 3 ft., 2½ x 4 ft., and 3½ x 5 ft. rugs along with short runners about 2½ x 6½ ft. There were hundreds of longer runners up to 25 ft. Practically all came with a design of repeated floral sprays and almost all had either red or ivory field (see Plate 33).

These rugs were medium to coarse in weave and had good heavy nap on cotton warp and weft. These were well suited to use in halls or on stairways where considerable color could be tolerated. This type was not finely woven but with its good wool such rugs gave good service, many wearing 30 to 60 years. They were popular and saleable rugs.

As a type Dergazine has all but disappeared from today's market, mostly replaced by less expensive florals from India. Older Dergazines often come from estate or tag sales and can be good values if in good condition.

DHURRIE RUGS
From India

Woven in northern India, Dhurries are flat-woven tapestry technique rugs generally of wool and cotton although some all cotton pieces are made. Designs are simple geometric patterns on plain background, although sometimes the Dhurrie will have crudely drawn figures of birds or animals as part of the design. Colors can range from soft pastels of green, blue, and rust through brighter tones. In the past several years decorators seem to have seized upon Dhurries and have promoted their use. Dhurries are very inexpensive, and the buyer should be wary of paying for a Dhurrie anything near the cost of a pile rug of similar size. A small Dhurrie might be satisfactory for a child's room or as an accent piece, but rarely will a large Dhurrie work well as a room-sized floor covering. Because they are much lighter than the coarsest pile rug they often wrinkle underfoot, and because of their construction they will not wear as well as even the most inexpensive pile carpet. Sizes range from scatters (3 x 5 ft. and 6 x 4 ft.) through about 10 x 14 ft.

"DORNA" QUALITY RUGS
From Rumania

The least expensive quality Oriental rug coming from Rumania. We have not purchased this grade and are not prepared to recommend it categorically. Still, with 45 to 50 knots per square inch these rugs are better than the thousands of cheap Turkish and Persian pieces once frequently featured by rug dealers. A Dorna quality rug in the right pattern and color would make an excellent utility rug for that high traffic area where a better rug would be inappropriate.

ENGSI BOKHARA RUGS
From Russia, Afghanistan, and Pakistan
(Sometimes called "Hatchli" or "Katchli" Bokharas)

This name indicates a particular rug design rather than a specific type of rug. In the Persian language "Katchli" means "cross" and indeed rugs in this design often have a field divided into four compartments by vertical and horizontal design elements which meet to form a sort of cross (see Plate 50 and 51). Perhaps because of the small arches sometimes woven at one end of these rugs, they were once considered to be a kind of Turkoman prayer rug. More recent investigation has revealed that rugs in this design seem to have originated for use as the innermost door cover or closure in a Turkoman yurt or felt tent. A more accurate name for the design is "Engsi"--the name used by the Turkoman themselves.

In size these pieces almost always measure about 6 x 4 ft. Rarely do they appear in sizes smaller than 3 x 5 ft. or larger than 5 x 8 ft. Because old pieces seem never to have been used on the floor by their makers, a surprising number apparently survived only to be worn thin and discarded in western households. New pieces in various qualities are available from Afghanistan and Pakistan.

ERSARI RUGS
From Russia and Afghanistan

Originally one of the Turkoman tribal groups, the name "Ersari" has been used by dealers to label a group of rugs coming from southern Russia (before World War II) and from Afghanistan. "Beshir" is sometimes used to indicate rugs of the same type. Ersari rugs come in a variety of sizes and styles, from mats and short runners through scatters and carpets. In general old Ersaris are thicker and less finely woven than Tekke, Chaudor, Salor, and other Turkoman types, while new Ersaris with their red grounds and repeated medallions can easily be confused with Afghan carpets. From time to time an old Ersari will come from an estate but most rugs of this type found in today's market would be new pieces from Afghanistan, and will be priced competitively with the better quality Afghan rug.

FERAGHAN RUGS
From Iran

None available and none imported from Iran since World War II, new or old. A good antique Feraghan is and has been a sought after collector's item since 1900. Not even from estates has one in saleable condition appeared. When one is found, it is usually so worn that it is practically worthless except for its art value. The collector who has one or two Feraghans in fairly good to excellent condition has irreplaceable rugs of great value.

Many lesser rugs in similar designs are available, however. Tabriz rugs often use the Feraghan design and old Tabriz have sometimes been represented as Feraghans. The "Feraghan" or "Herati" design consists of an allover lattice-like motif with small diamond center surrounded by four flanking curled leaves. Because of the angularity of the design the pattern is sometimes more geometric than floral in appearance. Rugs from many weaving areas have used this design down through the years (see, for example, Plate 10).

The collector looks for the old Feraghan with a green border of degenerate wool (the residual acidity in the green dye causes this color to erode prematurely like the black in some rugs, leaving the other colors embossed). Over the years hundreds of rugs from the Arak district (Mahals, Sultanabads, and Araks) and Hamadan district have been purchased as Feraghans. These rugs may have had the design of the old Feraghan but there was a vast difference in beauty and quality.

GEUNGE RUGS
From the Caucasus

Geunge is the name of one of the principal cities in Soviet Azerbaijan. As happened with other rug types the name of the market town was transferred to the types of rugs sold there regardless of where the rugs may actually have been woven or by whom. Geunge rugs often came in 4 x 7 ft. or 4½ x 8 ft. dimensions. Patterns were bold geometrics, sometimes with primitive animal or human figures, and colors primary tones of red, blue, green, gold, and ivory. Geunge rugs were usually of soft somewhat coarse weave, and nap was usually thick.

Old Geunge rugs sometimes still come from estates but condition is often poor. If in good shape, the Geunge will be as expensive as other Caucasian types. A more practical alternative today would be to consider one of the excellent Turkish types available.

GHIORDES PRAYER RUGS
From Turkey

No old Ghiordes have been imported since World War II. Antique Ghiordes prayer rugs are one of the dozen most collectible and sought-after of rug types by enthusiasts. Unfortunately, they are also one of the types to be most careful of. Many, many copies of old Turkish Ghiordes prayer rugs have been made in Turkey and elsewhere. Some of these copies are themselves old rugs today, and there is the danger of mistaking one of these rugs for an older and much more valuable Ghiordes.

The big development is the appearance in the last few years of a few new Turkish Ghiordes in the market. In the last few years we have been able to select some excellent new Ghiordes in the old colors and traditional prayer designs. As long as Turkish weavers are willing to make rugs in the quality of these selected pieces there will be a ready market for them.

GOREVAN RUGS
From Iran

Though many of these rugs from the Herez district are imported as Gorevans, all are offered by retail dealers as Herez. In the old days the name Gorevan was considered as good or better than Herez. The situation is now reversed. Today we class the Herez as a better quality rug than the Gorevan and most dealers offer all such rugs as Herez.

Gorevan is a village in the Herez district. Almost all rugs made there are in carpet sizes, 7 x 10 ft. or larger. Designs are usually geometric center medallion patterns and colors are usually in the red and blue family. These rugs have coarse to medium weave with cotton warp and weft and nap of excellent wool.

Very few Gorevans (or Herez) come to the U. S. today because of the high prices asked for them.

HAMADAN RUGS
From Iran

Many changes have occurred since the COMPLETE GUIDE first appeared in the 1960's, almost all of them adversely affecting the production of rugs in the Hamadan weaving district. Twenty years ago two out of three of the rugs imported to America were from the city of Hamadan and the surrounding district. Today very few rugs from this area are available. Child labor laws and high wages curtailed production in the early 1970's and the chaos of the Iranian Revolution in 1979 wiped out the market system that supplied most of the rugs for export.

Many varieties of rugs were woven in the Hamadan district with separate villages often making rugs of identifiable type. Bibikabad, Borchalou, Dergazine, Hosseinabad, Ingeles, Kapoutrahang, Kazvin, and several other major varieties of Hamadan rug can be identified by pattern and weave.

Most Hamadan types came in sizes from small mats up through large carpet sizes. Thousands of inexpensive 2 x 3 ft. mats and rugs up to 7 x 5 ft. were available in years past, along with thousands of runners. Most types were not fine and they were colorful, but they were good looking and durable as well (see Plate 32).

Hamadan goods are rare in today's market, forced out by the less expensive competition from Pakistan, India, and Rumania. Used Hamadan rugs will often be available from estates or at tag sales.

HATCHLI BOKHARA RUGS
From Russia, Afghanistan, or Pakistan
(See "Engsi Rugs")

HEREKE RUGS
From Turkey

A fine silk Hereke is possibly the very finest rug in weave to be had today. They were not on the market from 1920 until a few years ago. Woven in a small city near Istanbul, the choicest of these Hereke rugs will have 700 to 1200 knots to the square inch. Not surprisingly, prices are astronomical. If one has the means and owns many other rugs, he may want to add one of these, but the customer should be prepared to pay dearly.

Most silk Hereke rugs have very intricate floral designs, often with cream, champagne gold, or fawn backgrounds (see Plate 17). Hereke rugs are often identified as such by having the name "Hereke" woven in English in an outer border or lozenge. Good Hereke rugs often use metal brocade inlay in the field and border design as well. Be aware that some less expensive Turkish silks (principally Kayserei rugs) are sometimes offered as Hereke rugs at Hereke prices.

There are also some wool Hereke rugs to be found, sometimes of excellent quality, in patterns which remind one most often of allover Tabriz or Ghoum designs. Wool pile Herekes do not seem to appear often in commercial markets, however, and they are priced comparably with better quality city rugs from Iran.

HEREZ RUGS

FROM IRAN - So very plentiful in both new and semi-antique rugs fifteen to twenty years ago, now fewer and fewer are available at ever higher prices. For a long time the Herez was the least expensive carpet size rug from Iran available in a geometric pattern. Many, many Herez carpets have been sold in America in this century and today this type is frequently found at house sales and auctions, and for sale by dealers as semi-antique or antique. Most everyone with a bit of knowledge about Orientals is familiar with the design: a strong, angular central medallion with field covered with angular serrated leaves and stiffly drawn vines and blossoms (see Plate 13). Colors are often red and blue, although older Herez rugs sometimes have terra-cotta tones as the principal color with lighter accents of ivory and blue.

Very old Herez rugs seem to have been woven sometimes on wool foundation but all the Iranian Herez you could expect to find will be on cotton warp and weft. Weave is average, 60 to 70 knots per square inch in a good Herez, but the excellent wool made the type quite durable.

FROM INDIA - Many rugs are being made today in India in the Herez design. Some are lovely in color and most are available at a fraction of the price of an Iranian Herez. The production of Herez rugs in India will likely increase as time goes by. Most of these rugs are very saleable and good buys. They will, however, vary in grade according to the quality ordered by different importers. The price competition from these less expensive Indian Herez rugs has largely forced the Iranian type from the market.

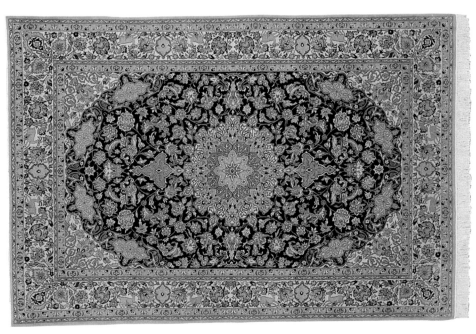

1. FINE NAIN IRAN 4' 1" x 6'
Very fine weave with closely clipped nap.
Cotton warp and weft, silk inlay in the field.

2. YALAMEH IRAN 3' 6" x 5'
Medium tight weave with warp and
weft of wool. Thick nap of excellent wool.

39

3. KASHAN   INDIA   6' 2" x 10'
Traditional pattern and color combination.
Fine weave, medium thick nap of excellent wool.

4. ISPHAHAN   INDIA   6' 4" x 9' 5"
Tight weave, thick nap of lustrous wool.

5. TABRIZ   INDIA   6' 7" x 9' 1"
Tight weave, thick nap of excellent
wool. Traditional figural animal design.

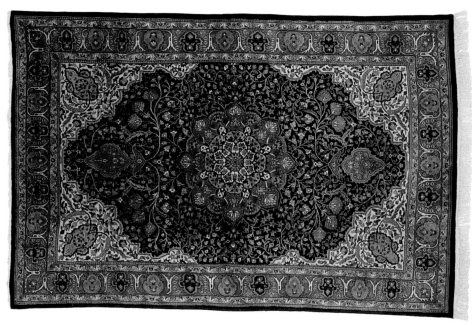

6. SAROUK   INDIA   6' 2" x 9' 5"
Tight weave, thick nap.

7. SAROUK   INDIA   4' 3" x 5' 11"
Tight weave, thick nap of good wool.
Traditional "Josan Sarouk" design.

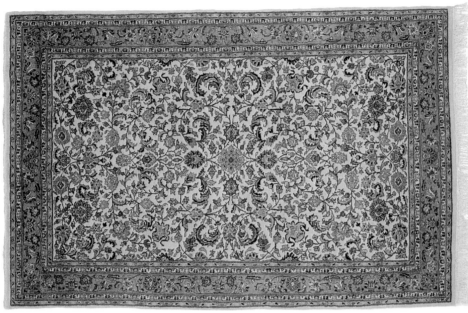

8. KASHAN   INDIA   6' 1" x 9' 3"
Medium fine weave, medium thick nap.
Classic "Shah Abbas" motif and color combination.

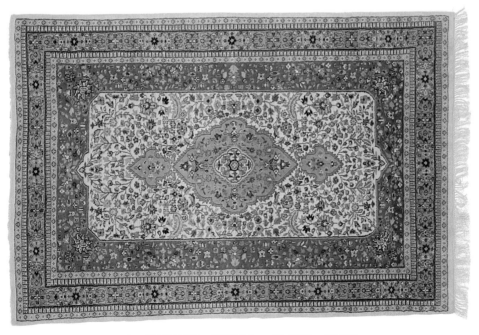

9. TABRIZ   INDIA   5' 10" x 8' 8"
Medium fine weave, thick nap of good wool.
"Book design" with elaborate inner border.

10. BIJAR   INDIA   4' x 5' 7"
Fine weave and thick nap with small scale "Herati" design.

11. SHIRVAN   INDIA   4' 2" x 6' 1"
Tightly knotted with medium thin nap
of lustrous wool. Old Caucasian "Akstafa" design.

44

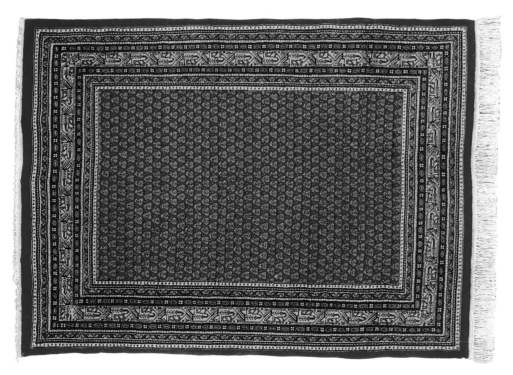

12. SARABEND   INDIA   4' 3" x 6'
"Mir" quality with tight weave and thick nap. All-over "boteh" design.

13. HEREZ INDIA 6' x 9' 6"
Medium weave with thick nap.

14. ABADEH INDIA
4' 3" x 6' 2"
Medium fine weave with
medium thick pile.

45

15. KASHAN PAKISTAN   4' 2" x 6' 2"
Fine weave with medium thick pile of especially select wool.

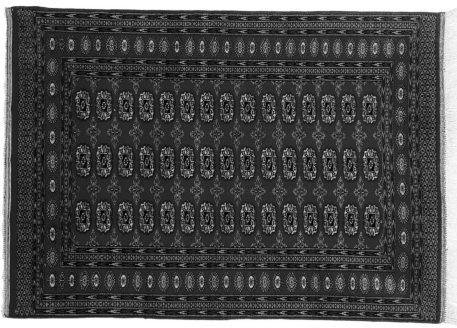

16. BOKHARA PAKISTAN   4' 1" x 6'
Fine weave ("12/24" quality) with closely clipped nap
of lustrous wool. Traditional "Tekke Bokhara" motif.

17. FINE SILK HEREKE   TURKEY   3' 10" x 6' 2"
Magnificent rug with extremely tight weave and
closely clipped nap. Silk foundation and pile with
areas of gold and silver metal brocade.

18. SHIRVAN TURKEY
4' 8" x 5' 7"
Old Caucasian design on wool
foundation. Medium thick pile.

19. KULA PRAYER TURKEY
3' 9" x 5' 6"
Medium tight weave with
thick nap. Wool warp and weft.

20. SHIRVAN TURKEY
3' 4" x 5'
Caucasian motif on
wool warp and weft.

21. SHIRVAN TURKEY
3' 8" x 5' 8"
Compact weave with medium
thick nap of excellent wool.

22. **BALOUCH PRAYER AFGHANISTAN**
2' 9" x 4' 5"
Typical Balouchi prayer
rug with medium fine
weave on wool warp and weft.

23. **AFGHAN AFGHANISTAN**
2' 6" x 4' 5"
Dense and compact
weave with medium thick
pile. Traditional colors and
Turkoman-derived design.

24. **ABADEH RUMANIA 5' 1" x 7' 9"**
Medium weave with medium-thick nap of excellent wool.

25. CHINESE   CHINA   4' x 6'
"90 line" quality with carved design in traditional motif.

26. SAVONNERIE INDIA
4' x 6'
French pattern from India.
Thick nap with carved design.

27. CHINESE   CHINA
3' x 5' 9"
New "antique finish"
rug in Art Deco style.
Medium weave, medium-thick nap.

50

28. KASHAN IRAN 4' 4" x 7'
Rich navy ground with red and ivory center and corners. Tight weave and closely clipped nap.

29. ISPHAHAN IRAN 5' x 7' 9"
Extremely tight weave with silk warp and weft. Closely clipped nap.

30. QUM IRAN 3' 7" x 5' 6"
Typical figural pattern. Wool pile with silk inlay.

31. SEMI ANTIQUE SAROUK IRAN 4' x 6' 1"
Old style pattern with red field. Often chemically washed and painted.

32. HAMADAN
IRAN 4' 1" x 6' 6"
Typical pattern and texture, here with a madder red field and navy border.

33. DERGAZINE
IRAN 3' 3" x 5' 2"
Typical floral Hamadan. Average weave, thick nap, red ground.

34. KASVIN IRAN 4' 6" x 6' 11"
Very thick nap, average weave, rich red field.

35. BIJAR IRAN 3' 4" x 5'
Stiff floral design, thick dense construction. Here with tomato red field.

36. ARDEBILE
IRAN 5' 5" x 7' 2"
Typical geometric motif. Cotton warp and weft; green, ivory, and rust colors.

37. SHIRAZ IRAN 5' 5" x 7' 2"
"Pole medallion" design, wool warp and weft. Rusty brown background.

38. KARAJA IRAN 2' 6" x 4' 9"
Medium-coarse weave, medium thick nap. Red background with navy, gold, and black.

39. AFSHAR IRAN 3' 9" x 5' 6"
Fine weave, closely clipped nap, wool warp and weft. Navy ground with gold, red, light blue, and rust.

40. ANTIQUE DAGHESTAN
CAUCASUS 4' x 5' 6"
Fine weave, closely clipped nap,
wool warp and weft. Navy ground
with gold, red, light blue, and rust.

41. ANTIQUE SHIRVAN
CAUCASUS 3' 7" x 4' 7"
Wool warp and weft, navy field
with soft greens and golds.

42. ANTIQUE KUBA
CAUCASUS 3' 9" x 6'
Fine weave, thin nap, wool warp
and weft. Navy with rich red, gold,
green, and light blue.

43. KULA PRAYER
TURKEY 4' x 5' 7"
Medium weave, medium thick nap, wool warp and weft. Burgundy red field.

44. KAYSEREI PRAYER
TURKEY 3' 9" x 5' 2"
Cotton warp and weft, medium thick nap. Soft green field with gold and ivory.

45. SHIRVAN PRAYER
TURKEY 3' 3" x 4' 3"
Modern Turkish rug in Caucasian motif. Rich gold ground.

46. KAZAK PRAYER
TURKEY 3' 2" x 5' 1"
Classic Caucasian design from Turkey. Wool warp and weft, red outer field.

47. KAFKAZI
PAKISTAN 4' 7" x 6'
Tight weave, medium-thin nap, cotton warp and weft.

48. PAKISTANI PRAYER
3' 1" x 5' 6"
Tight weave with thick nap.

Although most rugs from Pakistan come in Turkoman derived Bokhara designs, a variety of other patterns are found. "Kafkazi" rugs use geometric Caucasian motifs. These rugs often have tight weaves with very soft and lustrous wool nap. Prayer rugs are woven as well, often in a floral, fairly naturalistic style.

49. KAFKAZI
PAKISTAN 4' 4" x 6' 1"
Latch-hooked medallions, "serrated leaf and wine cup" border design.

50. ENGSI
AFGHANISTAN 5' 5" x 7'
A very fine new rug with silk foundation and closely clipped nap. Coppery brown ground with blue-black panels.

51. ANTIQUE TEKKE ENGSI
RUSSIA 3' 1" x 4' 4"
Tight weave with closely clipped nap. Rich mulberry red panels.

52. TABRIZ
RUMANIA 8' 5" x 10'
Old Tabriz animal motif, here with deep rust background.

53. HEREZ RUMANIA 4' x 6' 2"
Medium weave, medium-thick nap. Soft rust medallion and borders with gold, green, and navy accents.

HOSSEINABAD RUGS
From Iran

A variety of rug from the Hamadan District in Iran, Hosseinabads were generally good rugs although never finely woven. The great majority of them came with red field with small-scale Feraghan or Herati design in accents of green, navy, and ivory. Sometimes the design was employed as an allover pattern, sometimes a diamond-shaped central medallion in ivory or blue was added. Many small mats and 3½ x 5 ft. and 4½ x 7 ft. scatters came, as did thousands of runners in all lengths up to 25 ft. Today some used Hosseinabads will come from estates and will appear at tag sales, but few will be available from dealers.

HUNTING CARPETS
From India, Iran, and Rumania

These are rugs that have figural designs with deer and other animals and (generally) hunters on horseback portrayed amidst a floral setting. Except for the presence of hunters there is very little difference between a "hunting" and an "animal" carpet (see Plates 5 and 30). Many of the Taba-Tabaie Tabriz from Iran came with hunting and animal designs in the 1960's and 1970's. Most of the patterns are taken from designs found in 16th century rugs held by major museums. These patterns remain very popular today.

An animal or hunting rug is most attractive and usually a preferred design provided the animals and the hunters are well rendered and not out of scale with the scale of the rug. Such designs often come in different qualities. Thus two hunting rugs of equal size may differ considerably in price.

Hunting designs (and animal designs too) are used in many of the Orientals from India and Rumania. Once again, there is very significant price difference between a hunting rug from India and one from Iran of similar quality. Rumanian rugs are generally more expensive than Indian pieces, but are still much less costly than the Iranian carpets.

INDO-AUBUSSON
or
JEWEL OF KASHMIR RUGS
From India

These are flat stitched (not pile) rugs in the elaborate floral design and soft colors of the old French Aubussons. In texture and appearance these rugs remind one of needlepoint or crewel work. Almost a novelty item, we sold a few each year in the 1960's and early 1970's. Although decorative, they are not as fine as the old French Aubussons. They have also tripled in price in recent years and so most stores no longer stock them. They never were a volume seller, and were not suitable for heavy traffic.

INDO-PERSIAN RUGS
Rugs in Iranian Designs from India

The situation responsible for the appearance of so many Persian types from India is easy to explain. The disruptions in Iran in the last few years have drastically reduced the number of Iranian rugs available, while at the same time making such rugs so expensive that they can no longer be considered reasonable values. At the same time there is a growing interest in Oriental rugs in America (and around the world as well). More and more people realize how practical Oriental rugs are, yet are discouraged by the cost of some types of rugs. Many of these people appreciate the advantages of the pastel colored Savonnerie rugs from India that have been available for so long but prefer brighter colors and other patterns. Rugs from India in Iranian designs meet these needs perfectly.

Some dealers will continue to identify the rugs they offer as "Indo-Abadeh," "Indo-Sarouk," "Indo-Herez", etc., while others will describe them as "Abadeh from India," "Sarouk from India," etc. For information about the various Iranian design rugs from India one is likely to find offered today, please refer to the entry for the particular design.

INGELAS RUGS
From Iran

In the 1960's Ingelas rugs were available in good numbers in many sizes. This type was one of the best values available from the Hamadan District at that time. Almost invariably these rugs had a red background with allover small Feraghan design. Ingelas had one of the best and tightest weaves of all types from the Hamadan area.

None are available in the New York wholesale market today and it seems few are woven. Still available will be some used Ingelas scatters and runners from estates and from dealers who have taken them in trade.

This design has not often appeared among rugs from other weaving countries.

ISPHAHAN RUGS

FROM IRAN - The COMPLETE GUIDE gives complete information about the rather complicated history of this type. This is a name you can become easily confused about. Basically, there are three classes of rugs known by the name Isphahan. The first is a group of famous old antique carpets, almost all of which were woven prior to 1725. It is not definitely known where these early Isphahans were made, although they may actually be the product of weavers living in and around the city of Isphahan. The question is really only relevant for the hobbyist or collector interested in museums' holdings, for all of these oldest Isphahans are in the hands of large museums or wealthy collectors.

The second class of Isphahan rugs includes a large number of rugs exported from Iran beginning about 1900. These rugs were sold as Isphahans in Europe and America. Most were floral in design, and 9 x 12 ft. in size or larger. These "Isphahan" rugs were actually not made in the city of this name, but in the shrine city of Meshed several hundred miles to the east of Isphahan. The technical name for these rugs is Turkbaff. Very few of these rugs (many dealers call them "Isphahan-Mesheds") are imported today, but you might well find one at an estate sale or offered by a dealer as an antique or semi-antique Isphahan.

The third class of Isphahans consists of rugs woven in the city of Isphahan beginning in about 1920. Until World War II, most of these rugs were made in carpet sizes. Although quality was generally good, these Isphahans were not unusually fine in weave or materials. After the war quality increased dramatically, with many rugs made in classical medallion and floral patterns, some with weaves as fine as 700 knots to the square inch (see Plate 29). Recently Isphahans have begun to appear with silk warp and weft--the strong yet small diameter warp and weft allow for extremely tight knotting. It is sometimes difficult for the layman to tell these fine Isphahans from choice Nains or fine Qums.

Of course, rugs of this quality are very expensive even in smaller sizes. In the mid-1970's when it seemed to some people that Iranian rug prices would increase forever there was considerable speculative buying of these fine rugs. Rugs were purchased at wholesale with the hope they could be resold six months or a year later for a much higher price. Unfortunately for the speculators the big increase in price became self-limiting. As the wholesale price went higher, fewer and fewer rugs could be sold at retail, and so demand for such rugs decreased. There is no doubt that good numbers of fine Isphahan rugs remain in warehouses today with their owners still hoping for prices high enough to let them salvage their investment.

FROM INDIA- There are available some excellent Isphahan rugs and carpets in a variety of qualities from India. Most of the pieces we have selected are rugs with traditional curvilinear medallion and allover field designs (see Plate 4). Indian Isphahan rugs often have thicker nap than carpets from Iran of similar design, making the Indian rugs the more hard wearing of the two varieties. These are excellent rugs, most attractive in color and pattern, but they are not rugs with the 500 or 600 knots per square inch found in some Isphahans from Iran. There are some very finely woven Indian rugs available from Kashmir, but few of these pieces enter commercial channels (some are brought back to the United States by tourists who buy them in the shops where the tour buses stop).

FROM PAKISTAN - Some rugs of fine construction come from Pakistan in Isphahan design. With 250 to 350 knots per square inch and pile of lustrous and silky wool these Isphahans are fine enough for use as wall hangings, but durable and practical enough for use on the floor as well. Designs are often very elaborate and intricate, with delicate floral tracery and complex medallion, corner, and border treatments.

FROM RUMANIA - Occasionally we see Rumanian rugs with Isphahan designs. Usually found in carpet sizes of 8 x 10 ft. and larger these Isphahans often have the muted color tones characteristic of older rugs. They are an excellent choice for use with antique rugs and furnishings.

ISPHAHAN-MESHED RUGS
From Iran

Rugs by this name were actually woven in the city of Meshed. Most all pieces were in carpet sizes, and few if any have been imported from Iran in the past fifteen years. Some semi-antique pieces may come from estate sales but be careful to check condition carefully. Even an older Isphahan-Meshed in good condition should not be wildly expensive.

JOSAN SAROUK RUGS

FROM IRAN - This variety of floral, central medallion Sarouk was always popular and a good seller in America. In the late 1970's Josan Sarouks became very, very expensive, and sales plummeted as a result. An old one from an estate should be quite valuable. These carpets were thick and heavy with excellent wool. The navy and rich red which were the most typical colors did not appeal to all buyers, of course, but it was this kind of Sarouk that was largely responsible for the excellent reputation for durability and value still enjoyed by Sarouk rugs.

FROM INDIA - India has reproduced some outstanding Sarouk rugs in both scatter and carpet sizes. The best of these pieces are fully as desirable as a good Iranian Josan yet will cost several times less. It would be difficult for many laymen and some dealers to tell the difference between the Iranian and the Indian Josan (see Plate 7). In years to come there is little doubt these Indian Josan Sarouks will increase sharply in price.

JOSHIGAN RUGS

FROM IRAN - Most all Joshigan rugs and carpets come in a geometric pattern with angular blossoms and floral sprays on red backgrounds; some are found with navy or ivory fields. In the old days most Joshigan rugs were of average quality, but beginning in the mid-1960's there began to appear some very fine new rugs, Joshigans as finely woven as Kashans or carpet sized Isphahans. These tightly woven, closely clipped rugs were on cotton foundation, and varied in size from 2 x 3 ft. through 7 x 10 to 10 x 14 ft., although scatter sizes like 3½ x 5 ft. and 4 x 7 ft. seemed most plentiful. As might be imagined these fine Joshigans became very costly. Occasionally we still find one or two, but their high price limits their market.

FROM INDIA - Many rugs in Joshigan design come from India. In construction these scatters and carpets usually resemble the thicker, average quality Joshigans once available from Iran. Prices for these Indian Joshigans are very reasonable and they are very serviceable.

FROM RUMANIA - Some Joshigans from Rumania appear in both scatter and carpet sizes. Interestingly, Rumanian Joshigans often have fields of soft rust, terra cotta, or ivory in place of the red and blue that is typical of the Indian and Iranian rugs. As with other types, these Rumanian Joshigans are muted enough in appearance to meld well with old rugs.

KABISTAN RUGS

From the Caucasus
(See "Kuba" rugs)

KAPOUTRAHANG RUGS

From Iran

This was once about the least expensive of Iranian rugs in the 6 x 9 ft. and larger dimensions. As a rule new Kapoutrahangs were very bright and colorful, usually with red or ivory fields. They were coarsely woven but had good thick nap and wore fairly well. These were good values years ago, but at their present price they cannot compare with the much better quality rugs available for less money from India, Pakistan, and Rumania.

KARABAUGH RUGS
From the Caucasus

Karabaughs and Kazaks were two of the thicker and heavier varieties of rugs (as against thinner types like the Shirvan) made in the Caucasus. Many Karabaugh rugs used more floral forms than other Caucasians, although even these more curvilinear designs were stiff and conventionalized. A large "boteh" or pear shape is frequently a distinctive design element in the main field. Wool warp and weft.

In the absence of new Karabaughs from southern Russia or older pieces at reasonable prices the buyer is best advised to consider one of the fine Shirvans from the Jaipur area of northern India or one of the attractive village rugs from Turkey. While there is not a contemporary rug type which can be counted on to regularly use the old Karabaugh colors and designs, some of the Turkish scatters will come as close as can be found.

KARAJA RUGS

FROM IRAN - In the 1960's great numbers of Karaja rugs were available in mat sizes and runners like 2 x 3 ft., 2½ x 4 ft., 2 x 5 ft., and 2½ x 7 ft. Scatters also came in sizes like 3½ x 5 ft. and 4½ x 6½ ft. Qualities ranged from very coarse to average, with a few tightly woven pieces in the 4½ x 6 ft. size. A pole medallion arrangement with three angular medallions filling a central red field was most common for the scatters (see Plate 38). Accent colors could be light blue, yellow, gold, navy, and green. Because these rugs were so inexpensive they served well as utility rugs in areas of heavy use, and so often the used Karajas from estates will be somewhat thin. As a type Karaja has been yet another victim of the good quality non-Iranian rugs available to today's buyer.

FROM INDIA - Probably because of demand from the Germans rugs from Indian in Karaja design appeared early on, at least ten yers ago. Some of these Indian Karajas were hardly of better quality than the Iranian rugs they replaced (although the cost was considerably less), but in the course of time better quality Karajas have appeared. As always, regardless of county of origin name is no guarantee of quality: the buyer must always be prepared to judge the rug for himself.

KASHAN RUGS

FROM IRAN - For the customer with a taste for quality and a large enough budget the Kashan used to be the first choice in carpet sized Iranian rugs. Kashan came in two basic types, the traditional central medallion design with well filled field in red or (sometimes) navy blue and the so-called "Shah Abbas" style Kashan with ivory or cream or (sometimes) pale green background with all-over design of leaf, blossom, or vine arabesques (see Plates 3 and 8). Both types could be quite finely woven, and Kashans of both types usually had closely clipped nap of good wool. The close clipping of the pile helped show the crispness of the carpet's design to best advantage. Kashans were also available in scatter sizes (mostly 3½ x 5 ft. and 4½ x 7 ft.) but rarely in runner sizes and not often in small mats or 6 x 9 ft. dimensions.

Better quality Iranian Kashans reached record prices in the late 1970's and have not dropped since. With dealers asking five-figure prices for some 9 x 12 ft.

and 10 x 14 ft. carpets demand naturally slackened (there were less expensive "Aroon Kashans" sometimes found in the markets, but with coarser weave and wool and other materials of lower quality, they were never especially popular with most buyers).

FROM INDIA - As with a number of other types, India makes some excellent Kashans in both central medallion and Shah Abbas styles. How fine in weave depends upon what the dealer specifies and how much the customer is willing to pay. Most Indian Kashans will be thicker than their Iranian counterparts, and there is probably a greater variety of qualities from India than there were from Iran. Some dealers will choose less finely woven rugs to sell at a lower price while others will insist on more expensive pieces of better quality. Still, in even the best construction available from India the cost will be less than for an average good Iranian Kashan of comparable size.

FROM PAKISTAN - There are available some magnificent Kashans from Pakistan with fine weave and superb wool, pieces much better in quality than most Iranian rugs (see Plate 15). Prices for these pieces are much higher than for most Indian Kashans, but they are exceptional rugs. Sometimes small scatters are available, but a more typical size is 4 x 6 ft. or 5 x 7 ft. Carpets like 7 x 10 ft., 9 x 12 ft., and 10 x 14 ft. also appear. The supply of rugs of this excellent type is necessarily limited, and the dealer must examine each piece very carefully before the purchase.

KASHKAI RUGS

From Iran
(See "Shiraz," "Qashqai," "Mecca Rugs")

KASHMIR RUGS

From Kashmir, Northern India

A number of fine rugs in Iranian designs are woven today in Kashmir, most in scatter sizes up to 8 x 5 ft. Many of these are truly fine rugs, sometimes approaching the fine Nains and Isphahans from Iran in tightness of weave. Kashmir rugs are familiar to most dealers from pieces brought back by individuals who bought them there while on vacation or business. A few attempts have been made to import Kashmir rugs commercially but so far without much success. The Kashmir weavers are able to sell the limited numbers of rugs they make at a nice profit to tourists, and so dealers cannot afford to buy these and hope to sell them at a profit.

KASVIN RUGS

From Iran

Just before World War I there was begun in the city of Hamadan the production of rugs and carpets in more floral designs than had come previously from this area. These pieces were contracted for by European rug dealers in the same way we can contract for rugs in India today. Patterns most often resembled the elaborate central medallion designs from Kirman, although texture was not nearly as fine as a contract Kirman nor were colors as soft or as pastel as found in most later Kirmans. Kasvin rugs made up through the late 1960's usually had red or ivory backgrounds with large floral medallion, although occasionally rugs with navy fields were woven and sometimes all-over designs were made (see Plate 34). Foundation was always cotton, and with an average weave for a good Kasvin of about 100 knots per square inch this was a thick, heavy, and durable carpet.

Many dimensions were available with carpets in 6 x 9 ft., 8 x 10 ft., 9 x 12 ft., and larger sizes plentiful, as well as small mats and scatters and runners in shorter lengths.

After World War II there seemed some reduction in general quality especially of the wool used, but quality improved in the 1960's. With industrialization in the area of Hamadan prices rose rapidly and these ever higher costs drove most buyers to other rug types. A used Kasvin can be in excellent condition even after twenty or thirty years' use, and as thousands of Kasvins were sold in the United States market this is a type which would likely come from an estate or which might be found in a dealer's stock of used rugs. At a reasonable price a piece like this could be an excellent value.

KATCHLI BOKHARA RUGS

From Russia, Afghanistan, or Pakistan
(See "Engsi Rugs")

KAZAK RUGS

FROM THE CAUCASUS — Woven in an area northwest of Lake Sevan in what is today Soviet Armenia, old Kazak rugs are characterized by medium weave on wool warp and weft, thick heavy nap of excellent wool (the old Kazaks one sees today will often be worn right down to the foundation), and bold large scale geometric designs in primary colors of red, blue, and green with accents of gold, brown, and other shades. Dimensions are often chunky scatter sizes of about 6 x 7½ ft.

No old Kazaks have been imported since shortly after World War II and so the only source for such rugs has been from estates and occasionally from private collections. A choice piece in good condition is worth what the buyer will pay for it but an old Kazak that is badly worn is worth relatively little. Some buyers foolishly pay substantial prices for these worn out rugs. Some new rugs in Kazak design are apparently still woven in Soviet Armenia, but often the quality is not impressive and the high U. S. customs duty on these rugs have prevented them from creating much interest among buyers.

FROM TURKEY - A surprising number of contemporary scatter rugs from Turkey came in Kazak designs: classic triple medallion patterns, prayer designs, latchhooked central medallion, and compartmented field designs. The construction of these pieces is often strikingly reminiscent of old Kazaks even to the natural wool warp and red dyed wool weft. It appears that in a variety of cases Turkish weavers have taken their patterns from old Kazaks in collections or illustrated as color plates in rug books. Few rugs available today will be closer in spirit to the old Caucasians than some of these excellent Turkish types.

KELIM RUGS

From Iran, Turkey, Afghanistan

"Kelim" (a Turkish word) refers to the tapestry technique flat woven rugs made in many of the same areas that produce pile carpets. In a Kelim the design is constructed by varying the color of the warp and weft as the weaving progresses. The Kelim is usually reversible with the same design on front and back. Because the Kelim uses far less material than a pile rug and because it is usually quicker to produce the cost for a Kelim is far less than for a pile rug of equivalent size. The Kelim is much thinner, of course, and so less durable. As soon as the single thickness of warp or weft wears on the face the Kelim begins to look threadbare.

In the areas where they are made Kelims are used in a variety of ways: as floor coverings, as screens and awnings, as covers for miscellaneous bundles and packages, and in some areas even as shrouds for the dead.

Patterns are almost always simple geometric designs in primary colors, sometimes just an allover design.

Because they are not very satisfactory as a floor covering, the popularity of Kelims has been limited in America and Europe. Small Kelims can be quite decorative, however, and in the past few years interest in Kelims has grown on the part of both rug hobbyists and younger buyers, probably because Kelims can be much less expensive than some of the pile rug types (especially from Iran).

KHIVA OR KHIVA BOKHARA RUGS
From Russia and Afghanistan

"Khiva" occurs most often as an alternate name for an Afghan rug with allover design of large octagonal medallions or "guls." Today the name usually implies an Afghan of especially good quality.

KHURASAN RUGS
(Also spelled "Khorassan")
From Iran

Khurasan is the name of the large northeastern province of Iran having Meshed as its principal city and capital. A variety of rug types have been made in the area in the historic past but most types tended toward floral, curvilinear designs with richer, brighter colors than found in some other areas. Most Khurasan rugs came in carpet sizes. They were often well made and could be attractive, but sometimes the wool was not of the best quality. Khurasan rugs have not been available in any quantity since the late 1950's; as a type they will not be missed as there are more attractive carpets of better quality that cost less from India and Rumania.

KIRMAN RUGS

FROM IRAN - The area surrounding the city of Kirman in southern Iran has perhaps rivaled the Hamadan district in total rug output but the kinds of rugs produced are very different. Kirman always wove intricately floral rugs, and usually both weave and materials were excellent. In the early 1900's good numbers of well made rugs were available with realistic floral designs, allover vase motifs, and finely detailed leaf and vine designs, sometimes with birds and animals. By the 1920's and 1930's colors had become softer and Kirman rugs were generally thicker and heavier so as to better withstand the chemical bleaching that was now coming into vogue. By the 1950's most Kirmans brought to the United States were formal, floral, medallion designs with very soft and pastel fields of ivory, light blue, soft green, and rose. These carpets were often tightly woven, and they appealed strongly to buyers who were accustomed to the soft look of wall-to-wall carpeting. Kirman rugs with busier designs and more vivid colors continued to be made but most went to the European market.

One of the advantages of the way Kirmans were made--by contract--was that very large sizes could be found: 15 x 25 ft. carpets were not unusual, and even bigger pieces could be located.

By the mid-1960's the carpet factors in Kirman were in trouble. One of the largest visited us to bemoan the situation: his looms were full of partially completed Kirmans which had been begun at $1.00 a day labor rates. Weavers had demanded and received $3.00 a day, but were now threatening to leave the looms and the half finished rugs if he did not pay $5.00 a day. In India and Pakistan, of course, weavers continued to produce excellent quality carpets at the old cost (a cost, incidentally, fixed by their governments not by foreign carpet buyers). The disruption of the revolution of 1979 ended even the supply of high priced Kirmans. Most better quality Kirmans were contract rugs, and no buyer would take the chance of contracting for rugs he very probably would never receive.

Unlike some dealers we were never overly impressed with the chemically treated Kirmans which came to America in such numbers from 1925 on. Although tightly woven and with thick nap they did not give the service other untreated Orientals did, and they did not retain their value well. The fairly cheap bazaar quality Kirmans which were brought to the United States as a less expensive alternative to the more costly contract rugs were even worse. Unless purchased for a very reasonable price even a used Kirman in good condition can be a questionable value.

FROM INDIA - India produces a variety of types which compete directly with the Iranian Kirman. Not only are there rugs from India in the Kirman designs, but Indian rugs in Tabriz and Isphahan patterns often have the soft and muted color tones and formal, floral designs sought in Kirmans in years past. The much lower prices of these Indian carpets hastened the end of large scale Kirman production.

KIR-SHEHR RUGS
From Turkey

Excellent small prayer rugs came from this small city before the turn of the century. A distinctive striped border is often found and prayer rugs in the 3½ x 5 ft. and 6 x 4 ft. sizes also occur. Some runners are also found. Colors were most often a distinctive shade of grass green with magenta as a secondary hue. Wool was usually soft and glossy. Very few if any old Kir-Shehr rugs will be found today, but rugs are still woven in the area, some in the old designs and colors. A new rug of this type could well be an antique of the future.

KONIA RUGS
From Turkey

South of Ankara and about 65 miles from the Mediterranean is the large city of Konia. In the old days numbers of rugs seem to have been woven in Konia although few reached markets in the West. Colors were usually limited to golds, browns, and yellows, with a particular piece sometimes having a soft pale apricot or light blue field. Prayer rugs had an interesting arrangement with the prayer arch usually centered in the field, leaving an unusually large upper spandrel which often held geometric leaf forms. Weave was not fine but the wool was outstandingly soft and lustrous.

While few buyers will even have the chance to see an old Konia in good condition there are new rugs available in the colors and patterns of older pieces. Like the older rugs sizes can range from 3 x 4 ft. through 4 x 8 ft. There are no large carpets.

KUBA RUGS
From the Caucasus

"Cabistan," "Kabistan," and "Kuba" rugs are one and the same type. These are finely woven, short napped rugs with strong and often intricately detailed geometric designs (see Plate 42). None have been imported to the United States since about 1935, and many of the Kubas once in American hands were purchased for the German market in the 1950's, 60's and 70's. Particularly rich blues, reds, and golds sometimes occur and often the juxtaposition of colors is striking. Various Kuba types have been identified, for instance the "Seichur" style with cross motif or stylized flowers in an allover pattern, or the "Perpedil" motif with allover geometric design featuring stylized rams' horns and bird figure designs. An old Kuba in prime condition is a rare and valuable rug.

FROM TURKEY - From time to time Turkish pieces appear in Kuba designs, although not as frequently as in Kazak patterns. Turkish rugs do not often have the jewel-like color intensity of old Kubas and often are not as fine in weave as the old pieces. Still, interesting examples come and might interest the potential buyer.

FROM INDIA - Some of the well made rugs from the Jaipur area of India appear in Perpedil and other Kuba designs. These Indian rugs are tightly woven with closely clipped nap and so the intricate design is well rendered. An Indian Perpedil of this kind would cost one-tenth the price of an average quality Kuba.

KULA RUGS
From Turkey

Rugs have been woven in the vicinity of Kula (south of Ghiordes and due east of Izmir) for several hundred years; older pieces have long been in demand by rug hobbyists. Old Kulas and especially old prayer Kulas are sometimes hard to differentiate from old Ghiordes as they share somewhat similar designs and color tonalities. Kula rugs often have soft golden browns, apricot, gold, blue, and muted reds and greens. A prayer Kula usually has a more or less open field (although not as open as most Ghiordes prayers) in gold, blue, or red with flanking columns and upper spandrel densely covered with a stylized repeated blossom design. Often an elongated floral spray takes the place of the stylized lantern found just below the prayer arch in some prayer rugs. As with many kinds of Turkish rugs, borders are wide and important to the design. Non-prayer Kulas often have corner brackets joined together to form a sort of double spandrel effect, with central field having stylized floral sprays. Old Kulas have not been imported for 60 years and pieces in good condition are rarely available. Good older Kulas were beyond the budget of most antique rug buyers in 1920.

Among the new Turkish rugs available today Kulas are found in both prayer and non-prayer designs. New pieces are often very well made with weaves of 80 to 100 knots per square inch, wool warp and weft, and thick nap of good quality wool. As with older Kulas most new rugs come in sizes from about 4 x 5½ ft. through 5 x 7 ft.

In today's market "Kula" is sometimes used to indicate a particular quality of Turkish rug, as "a Ghiordes or Kazak in Kula quality."

KUM KAPU RUGS
From Turkey

For different periods over the past several hundred years rugs of especially fine quality have been made in the vicinity of Istanbul. Always made in a work-shop setting these rugs were intended to be the very finest quality skilled weavers could produce. Professional designers made the patterns and the extensive use of silk and silver and gold brocade was common. Sizes were usually small, 3 x 5 ft. to 4½ x 6½ ft. Rugs of this variety woven in the mid to late 1800's are often called Kum Kapu. In nearly 60 years in the trade Colonel Jacobsen can recall handling only three such pieces. Today the very best of the Hereke rugs from Turkey carry on this tradition of extraordinarily fine and expensive silk and metal inlay weaving.

KURDISH RUGS
From Iran

Kurdish rugs include so many types from such a large geographic area--including not only a large part of western Iran but a section of eastern Turkey as well--that it is difficult to avoid generalities. As a people the Kurds share a culture and language that sets them apart from other Persians, and their rugs too are identifiable even if it is impossible to say exactly where they were woven. Up until the 1930's and the coming of World War II some Kurds remained true nomads following their flocks from the lowlands in the winter to the high summer pastures. Other Kurds lived in villages or towns and were exposed to rugs woven in other areas by non-Kurdish peoples.

Most often Kurdish pieces were rather thick rugs with average good weave to rather loose weave, but generally with superb quality wool as the pile material. Few rugs are more beautiful than a choice old Kurd, for these rugs often had the lovely natural sheen that is the mark of superior wool. Usually Kurdish rugs were woven on woolen warp and weft, although in some villages (as around Hamadan) cotton might be used as a foundation material. Most Kurdish rugs came in scatter and runner sizes although once again larger carpets might be woven in a village. Patterns tend toward strong geometrics and rich primary colors although sometimes rugs with more curvilinear floral designs were woven.

Few new Kurdish rugs have been available in the market for years, but older rugs sometimes come from estates. The Reza Shah forcibly settled many Kurds into villages in the 1920's and 30's, but with the abdication of the last Shah of Iran the Kurds may have more autonomy than in past decades, and this may encourage continued and renewed rug production.

LADIK RUGS
From Turkey

The choice old Ladiks and prayer Ladiks rank with the rare Ghiordes and Kulas in beauty and value but seldom does a good old Ladik appear today even from an estate or collection.

In style the old Ladiks often had rich red, or blue, or sometimes canary yellow or golden yellow grounds. Prayer rugs often had a divided field with a large lower panel decorated with van dykes and pomegranates. Sizes were always small, ranging from about 4 x 6 ft. to 4½ x 7 ft.

Some rather good quality Ladiks with nice colors are woven today in Turkey in the old patterns. Few of the rugs compare with the best of the 19th century production but they are practical rugs that can be used as everyday furnishings.

LARISTAN RUGS
From Iran and India

In the 1920's and 30's a few rugs from Iran were imported and offered as "Laristans." These rugs in scatter sizes resembled Bahktiari or Shiraz rugs of the period: the name was very indefinite.

In contrast, Laristans from India were a well recognized type. Of about the texture and thickness of an Iranian Kirman these Laristans were contract rugs made in two basic qualities. Most were carpets and most had a strawberry-rose field or a background of creamy, golden tan. Designs were usually copies of the well known vase carpets in the Metropolitan in New York and Victoria and Albert Museum in London. As a type these carpets were more durable than the chemically treated Kirman. Production seems to have ended about 1933.

LILLIHAN RUGS
From Iran

While some new rugs of this type did come up through the 1960's not many have been imported since World War II. Found in both scatter and carpet sizes, Lillihans were invariably in a Sarouk-like design with detached floral pattern and usually with red or rose background. From 1920 until World War II 99% of these Lillihans were chemically washed and painted to give the look of an older rug. Lillihans of the period were sometimes called the poor man's Sarouk. Nevertheless they were one of the most popular of types before World War II and the biggest seller in the large stores that handled chemically washed and painted rugs.

Not seen in the wholesale market today, a Lillihan might come from an estate or as a trade-in. Most will be well worn and worth very little.

MAHAL
From Iran

Large numbers of Mahal rugs came to the United States up through the 1950's and early 1960's. All were in carpet sizes, most in 9 x 12 ft. and 10½ x 14 ft., although some 7½ x 10½ ft. and large 11 x 17 ft. carpets were found. "Mahal" implied a particular quality of rug from the Arak district rather than a type that differed in basic structure or color or pattern from other Arak types. The best of the Araks (except for Sarouks) were called Araks by most dealers; next best were Sultanabads, then came Mahals, then Muskabads. Most Mahals had medium thick nap of rather loose weave with floral, allover designs. Few older Mahals in carpet sizes will be found without some worn areas after forty years' use.

MECCA SHIRAZ RUGS
From Iran
(See "Qashqai Rugs")

MEHREBAN RUGS
From Iran

Herez rugs of especially good quality are often offered as Mehrebans regardless of what village actually produced them. As might be expected, a Mehreban is even more expensive than an Iranian Herez of average quality, a type already much more costly than the good carpets available from Rumania and India in Herez design.

MELEZ RUGS
From Turkey

An old one is one of the rarest of antique rugs. A good one is a prize collector's item. The antiques were in both prayer and non-prayer designs.

The prayer design had a bottle-neck prayer arch somewhat separated from the main field by triangular intrusions creating a sort of head and shoulders effect. Sizes ranged from about 5 x 3 ft. to 6 x 4 ft. The field was almost always tawny red (almost a salmon) with the area above the arch in ivory. The main border invariably was yellow or canary with the turtle design always in a deep lavender. Once having seen one of these you should always recognize another. Unfortunately the chances of seeing an old prayer Melez in a rug store are slight. Only in museums and only in private collections will you find one, and then only in collections made forty or more years ago. The typical non-prayer Melez is a design also easy to recognize. Many have a central field divided into vertical strips, each strip having a repeated guard border design.

The good news is that for the first time in sixty years new Melez rugs in both prayer and non-prayer designs and in the colors of the antique Melez are being made in Turkey. Such rugs vary in sizes up to about 7 x 5 ft. Many are of excellent quality, still woven on woolen warp and weft as were the old pieces.

MESHED RUGS
From Iran

There are many types and qualities of rugs woven in the Khurasan District of Iran and in and around the city of Meshed. Several names have been used for rugs from this area: Meshed, Turkbaff, and Khurasan are common. Numbers of better quality Mesheds were sold in years past as "Isphahan-Mesheds." Some were simply offered as Isphahans.

Practically all the Meshed area rugs that came to America were in carpet sizes. The best of these, the Turkbaffs, were attractive rugs with floral designs and medium to sometimes somber color combinations of red, blue, pink, brown, green, and ivory. The average Meshed had bright colors and was not a very durable rug. The cochineal red grounds often seemed to wear prematurely.

Mesheds seldom come to America today because of price. The best type to come from this area in recent years was the Mood, a variety with good weave and materials but a type still more expensive than Meshed (see the entry under "Mood" for more details). In general Mesheds were less expensive rugs that sold for price. They have been replaced by better but less expensive types from other weaving countries.

"MILCO" QUALITY RUGS
From Rumania

This is the name of one of the finer rug qualities coming from Rumania. Milco grade has 194 knots to the square inch. Many sizes (up to 13 x 16 ft.) and designs (Tabriz, Isphahan, Kashan) are made in this grade. Warp and weft is cotton, and the wool used is of fine quality. The Senna knot is used.

MING RUGS
From China

The name is used for those rugs dating from the Ming Dynasty. Few rugs remain from that period. Those which do are not finely woven and are all rather thin rugs with good wool quality. Old rugs from the Ming period have never been available commercially.

Since World War II there have been many rugs imported from India, some in these old Ming designs, some simply in a Chinese design but using this name. More often than not, however, the name implies nothing more than a rug in traditional Chinese design, whether from China, India, or Taiwan.

MORI RUGS
(also spelled "Mauri")
From Pakistan and Afghanistan

When the Bokhara rugs from Pakistan first became available in numbers in 1955, the dealers in Pakistan and London referred to most of these as "Mori" rugs. They were found in all sizes and usually in the typical Bokhara design. These were not the superb heavy Karachi quality. Most were a thinner Lahore quality. Thus "Mori" is a somewhat dated general name once applied to these Bokhara types. Today we refer to such rugs as "Pakistani Bokharas in the Lahore quality."

Afghanistan still produces many excellent rugs called "Mauri" carpets. These are usually in the old Tekke Bokhara designs. The Afghan Mauris are excellent rugs, firmly woven on woolen warp and weft. They have perhaps the best wool of any type made in Afghanistan today. Again note that they usually use the small Tekke octagon, not the big Ersari Afghan octagon. They are made in many sizes up to 9 x 12 ft. with perhaps some few larger sizes as well.

MOSUL RUGS
From Iran

See COMPLETE GUIDE. You can forget this name: they were among the coarsest and cheapest of all Persian rugs marketed in Hamadan. They came in sizes about 6 x 3½ ft. and in many old Hamadan designs. The poorest of all was the Zendjian Mosul but these have not come to America since World War II and the vast majority have worn out and been discarded. No one will mourn the passing of this type.

MUSKABAD
From Iran

The lowest quality carpet size rugs from the Arak area in central Iran. Many carpets were imported as Muskabads up through the 1950's but the better rugs were sold as Sultanabads or Mahals. No new Muskabads are available in today's market, and an old one will usually be in poor condition.

NAIN RUGS
From Iran

One of the three finest types of rugs woven in Iran in the last 100 years. Few of the rugs of the past 300 years were so finely woven. Only the finest new Isphahans with silk warp and some of the all silk Ghoums are so finely woven with 500 to 600 knots to the square inch. Most Nains are made in approximately 8 x 5 ft. size (with some 3 million hand-tied knots). A Nain of this size required the labor of two people for two years. Others are approximately 5 x 3 ft. in size with some smaller made, and a few in 7 x 10, 9 x 12, 10 x 14 ft. and occasionally even larger sizes. Practically all are in soft shades on ivory or blue field. Some few do appear with red background or even green field. The intricate foliage is frequently outlined with silk inlay.

Photographs do not do this rug justice (see Plate 1). Available in good numbers up to 1972—now much more scarce and sharply up in price over those fifteen years ago. Most new rugs were pieces woven on contract in Iran. Because they were so finely made and took so long to produce no individual weaver could afford to begin such a rug because there would be no income for him until the rug was completed and sold a year or two in the future. Instead an entrepreneur would arrange for the making of the rug. Usually a professional designer was hired to draw a cartoon for the rug's pattern while another workman made a graph from the cartoon. The use of a graph makes possible the intricate design characteristics of such fine city rugs. The weaver worked directly from the graph, and the contractor arranged to pay him at regular intervals for his labor. Even before the rug was completely finished buyers could inspect it and perhaps buy it—often at a somewhat lower price than if the rug were completed before being sold (because the contractor would have his profit quicker).

With the abdication of the Shah in 1979 this complicated system of contracting for rugs in Iran pretty much ended. Many Iranians with foreign connections left the country fearing the changes a very conservative religious government would bring. Instead of making fine rugs that would take several years to finish (and which would be worthless if the weaver was forced to stop work half way through) more coarsely woven rugs were begun.

Numbers of fine Nains are still available outside Iran, but prices are extremely high because the continued supply of such rugs is uncertain. It is impossible to predict with assurance what will happen in the future, but it seems clear that as long as conditions remain unsettled in Iran there will be few very fine new rugs woven there.

NIRIS RUGS
From Iran

No antique or new rug by this name has been imported since 1930. Woven near Niris in southern Iran all were in dozar sizes about 4 x 6 ft. and most were in ivory backgrounds with floriated pear design with green predominating. Most had tightly woven multicolored selvages and multicolored overcasting of sides. The new Persian Abadeh is nearest in texture to this type.

"OLT" QUALITY RUGS
From Rumania

"Olt" indicates a particular quality of Rumanian Oriental, not the name of a rug type or design. Olt grade rugs are tightly woven, with 160 knots per square inch and medium thick nap of excellent wool. A variety of floral and some geometric designs are found in this qualtiy, and rugs in Olt quality are available from scatter sizes through large carpets.

OUSHAK RUGS
From Turkey

A famous type of antique Turkish rug whose name has lately been very much abused. Old "Star Oushaks" (named for the star-like medallions that fill their fields) are very rare; numbers of these rugs in large sizes went to Europe in the 16th, 17th, and 18th centuries. In furnishing rugs for Williamsburg an Oushak was chosen for the Governor's mansion because that was one of the types of Turkish rug that could be shown to date to that period.

A choice antique Oushak has seldom appeared from a European collection in the past fifty years. After World War I the cheapest and poorest of Turkish Anatolian carpets were given this name. In the past few years a few dealers have offered numbers of rugs as Oushaks. It seems almost any old Turkish carpet they find is given this name. These "Oushaks" can be truly horrible rugs, coarse in weave and with the bad dyes that marked the nadir of Turkish weaving. It would be interesting to find out where the old "Oushaks" one sees offered come from. In the past 60 years Col. Jacobsen never saw many available; no importer had them nor were they found in government warehouses in Turkey for the last half century.

PINDE RUGS
From Russia and Afghanistan

A very rare type of antique Bokhara from Central Asia usually in small carpet size and often of excellent weave, sometimes with areas of cotton or silk used as accent in the wool field. Some few new Turkoman rugs from Russia as well as some new rugs from Afghanistan are called Pindes, but these are nothing like the old ones. "Pinde" is loosely used today to indicate a Turkoman rug of especially good quality.

POLONAISE CARPETS
From Iran

This type name is given to a group of antique floral, finely woven silk rugs with metal inlay of gold or silver brocade. Many of the existing rugs of this type (about 300 examples) were collected in Europe, especially in Poland (hence the name for the type). Examples seem to date to the 17th century and a bit earlier. Without question these rugs were woven in old Persia, and over the years Isphahan has been suggested as the most likely source for them.

PRINCESS BOKHARA

"Princess Bokhara" is an invented name usually applied to Turkoman rugs in the Engsi (or Hatchli) design. There was and is sometimes confusion and misinformation about the origin of particular rug types, and invented names of this sort are not uncommon. Such names were useful insofar as they were understood by others but better scholarship is available today and there is an effort on the part of most reputable dealers to describe their goods as accurately as possible.

QASHQAI RUGS
From Iran

The Qashqai are a people living in the Fars province of southern Iran. Up until the 1920's and 1930's many were true nomads, traveling with their flocks and draft animals from the high pastures in the summer to the warmer coastal lowlands in the winter. Of all the weavings of Fars, some of the Qashqai types have been generally judged superior. Often called "Qashqai Shiraz" rugs, the workmanship could be excellent, with very fine weave and intricate geometric designs in rich vegetable colors. In good Qashqai rugs the wool is exceptional, very lustrous and soft yet long staple and very strong.

A particular type of Qashqai rug in an unusually naturalistic millefleur design with a "mehrab" or prayer arch (the design was probably taken from a pattern which originated in India) was called "Mecca Shiraz" by many dealers. Elaborate stories were sometimes concocted to connect these beautiful rugs from southern Iran with the Holy City of Mecca in Saudi Arabia.

Because until 50 years ago most all Qashqai Shiraz rugs were woven by people perpetually on the move, sizes were always small, seldom larger than 7 x 10 ft. These rugs were woven on simple horizontal looms which limited the dimensions possible.

Under the Reza Shah and his son, the last Shah of Iran, the mobility of the Qashqai was severely limited. Many were settled in villages and towns and as their way of life changed, the general quality of their weaving deteriorated. Oil wealth and development in the south brought a different economy and much higher labor costs in the 1960's and Qashqai rugs became very much more expensive than previously. Other Fars types continued to come, but all became less and less competitive with rugs from other weaving countries.

QUM OR GHOUM RUGS
(Also spelled "Gum," "Ghum," "Goum")
From Iran

Qums (Ghoums) are one of the three finest and costliest types of Iranian rugs. Most are in small to scatter sizes up to about 5 x 8 ft., but a limited number were available in sizes up to 9 x 12 ft. In the recent past a good number of Qums were woven with silk pile on silk foundation. Most of these are 2 x 3 ft. to 4 x 6 ft. sizes. They are as finely woven as the Nains and Isphahans and are very exquisite rugs . . . and also very expensive.

The Qums of recent years are much more finely woven and much more beautiful in design than the Qums of the thirties, or even those rugs woven prior to 1965. The designs of many of the early ones were disturbingly unusual and the rugs themselves were not nearly as fine in weave as those coming today. Like Nains and fine Isphahans, most Qums were contract rugs. With the changes in Iran since 1979, few if any new fine Qums are woven. Costs are very high today and the market very unsettled.

ROYAL BOKHARA RUGS
(See "Tekke Rugs")

Tekke rugs have been called "Royal Bokharas" for over a hundred years by dealers, hobbyists, and rug enthusiasts. Older rug books often rhapsodize about magnificent "Royal Bokharas." Like "Princess Bokhara" one will sometimes still find a dealer who talks about "Royal Bokharas," although what he means to describe is a Turkoman or Turkoman style rug in the typical Tekke design with multiple rows of small octagonal "guls" or medallions (see Plate 16).

SALOR RUGS
From Russian Turkestan

The Salor tribes were said to be the most aristocratic of all the Tukoman tribes. The rugs they wove all came in some shade of red field with two or more rows of small elongated octagons--each octagon was generally surrounded by a geometric latchhooked border. Most fine Salors came as tent bags about 2½ x 4 ft. in size. They were much sought after by rug collectors.

Colonel Jacobsen bought scores of the finest and oldest of these in the early 1930's in the London warehouses as the Russians sent huge rug shipments abroad to raise cash. None have appeared in commercial channels, however, since World War II. A number were made in long narrow tent bag sizes like 4 to 5 ft. long by 12 inches to 2 ft. wide. A very few came in slightly larger sizes about 6 x 3½ ft. Perhaps some few of these Salors will reappear should business become a bit easier to carry on with Russia in the future.

SAMARKAND RUGS
From Central Asia

Very little space need be devoted to this rug. No antique Samarkands have been imported or seen in the European markets since World War II. Those that we saw and bought then were among the coarsest and flimsiest of all rugs. Even the antiques of 1875 - 1925 were very coarse in weave--yet even so, the collectors of the day wanted one. In Chinese-like motifs a typical Samarkand rug had unusual combinations of colors, i.e., canary, orange, tawny reds, some blues, greens, and ivory. A good one had exquisite silk-like wool and patina, and yet was very coarse and thin. All were in small sizes to about 6 x 10 ft.

SARABEND RUGS

FROM IRAN - The Sarabend design--the small "pear" or paisley pattern--is very well known. The design was long associated with the town of Sarawan some thirty miles from Arak and not distant from Hamadan itself. The choicest antique type was the Mir-Sarabend, often referred to simply as a "Mir." No true Mir-Sarabends have been imported in the past fifty years. They were always in scatter and runner sizes.

The typical Sarabend with the small pear design on a rose or red field and ivory border in sizes 4 x 2½ ft. to 5 x 3½ ft. and 7 x 4½ ft. came in good numbers up through the early 1970's. Right after World War II many semi-old rugs were included among newer rugs in most shipments. The new ones were very good until about 1960 when the quality became much worse. The best rugs in the typical Sarabend design were the Sarabend Sarouks--a superior rug which became over-expensive as labor costs increased in Iran. At the same time the quality of most Sarabends was lowered. The Sarabend from Iran will not be greatly missed.

FROM INDIA - Indian weavers have perhaps been most successful of all with the Sarabend design, and the best of the new Indians are finer in wool and weave than the best Iranian Sarabends. In addition these Indians have nicer color than most Iranian Sarabends of the past ten years and actually have nicer colors than the majority of new Iranian Sarabend Sarouks. These better Sarabends are often called "Mir Sarabends." Sarabends today from India are available in a wide variety of qualities from quite inexpensive rugs to pieces with tight weave and excellent wool which are more costly. Even the best Mir Sarabend from India is much less expensive than a mediocre Iranian rug.

SARABEND-SAROUK RUGS
From Iran

Shortly after World War II the Sarabend Sarouk rug made its first appearance. The Germans initiated this development. These rugs were all in the typical Sara-bend design, i.e., the small repetitive pear design covering the entire field and with the Sarouk weave and quality (see Plate 12). Actually in the beginning most of these were better woven, better quality rugs than the typical Sarouk of the same period with the allover detached floral design. Most came in red field, but a good many also came in ivory. Some also came in navy, gold, and light blue background. They were made in many sizes from 3 x 5 ft. to 12 x 20 ft. carpets. About 1972 inflation in Iran reduced the quality and also sent prices up sharply. Only the insistent Persian rug seeker will pay the price for one of these when the Sarabends from India are so beautiful and of such excellent quality at half the price of the Iranian type.

SAROUK RUGS

Sarouk has been perhaps the best known name among Iranian rug types for the last 60 years. This is not to imply that Sarouks are better rugs than other types, but simply to recognize their great popularity among both European and American buyers.

FROM IRAN - The important point to note is that in the years from 1910 to about 1960 nine out of ten Sarouks from Iran were both chemically bleached and redyed ("washed and painted" in the language of the trade). The process was designed to give new rugs the color balance and look of older rugs, but the customer paid a double penalty: to have a rug washed and painted made it more expensive, and a washed and painted rug would not wear as well as an untreated rug nor would it be worth as much in years to come. Notwithstanding the washing and painting of these rugs (see below for hints on detection), the Sarouk was generally regarded by the public as being one of the best types available. More Sarouks were sold than any other single type of Iranian rug excepting the less expensive scatters from the Hamadan district and from the area around Herez.

The vast majority of all Sarouks were in an allover floral design introduced around 1905 to please American decorators who wanted floral rugs in carpet sizes (see Plate 31). Up until about 1965 when the Germans came to dominate the rug market in Iran there were huge stocks of rugs in this allover design available. Rugs with red, rose, or plum fields in all sizes from 2 x 3 ft. through giant carpets were easy to find. Hundreds of 9 x 12 ft. Sarouks could be examined in New York at all times. By 1980 not 1% of the Sarouks previously available were to be found in the market. Ever higher prices led customers to buy other types which were better values.

Two other Sarouk varieties:

After World War II there came on the market two other types of Sarouk from Iran. The Sarabend Sarouk with the small allover pear design in the image of the old Sarabend rugs first appeared in the mid-1950's. These Sarabend Sarouks were better than any Sarabends of the previous fifty years, and were often of better quality than the allover design Sarouks of the same period. The Germans, who disliked the allover floral design, were responsible for introducing the Sarabend pattern. These rugs came overwhelmingly in rose or red field, but some also came in navy, ivory, or even light blue fields. Most Sarabend Sarouks had the allover "boteh" or pear design, but some added a central medallion and corner brackets while in a very few rugs the field was a plain solid color, empty of design. Sizes ranged from 2½ x 4 ft. through large carpet sizes.

The other type of Sarouk which the Germans must be given credit for is the Josan Sarouk. It employs an old Isphahan pattern, usually combining the Shah Abbas motif of allover floral vines, leaves, and blossoms with a medallion (see Plate 7). The background of these Josans was generally ivory, soft rose, or red. A limited number of carpet sizes appeared with blue field. Many of the smaller Josan Sarouks in 2 x 3 ft. (about the best of all small rugs in the years from 1950 to 1970) to 7 x 4½ ft. sizes had blue fields. The Josan Sarouk was perhaps the best of the three types of Sarouks available in this century. Today, all of these types of Sarouks have practically disappeared from the market. Very few are made and those that are available are incredibly high priced.

A word of caution about washed and painted Sarouks: since you as a customer will not be offered many new Sarouks imported from Iran today or in the future, you may make the mistake of paying a big price for a used Sarouk from a dealer or at an estate sale. Surely you will not bid on a Sarouk at an auction. Since almost all of the Sarouks imported to America between 1910 and 1960 were chemically washed and painted the odds are that any used Sarouk you see will be so treated. The owner might say, "My mother's Sarouk can't be treated because she bought it in 1925" but that's when most Sarouks and over 50% of all Persian rugs were chemically treated.

Many ask how to tell if a rug was chemically washed and painted. Any one of our employees can tell almost at a glance because the rug will usually have unnatural color tones, but colors are difficult to judge without the chance to examine and compare hundreds of rugs. In our showroom we have several small washed and painted rugs that we use to point out the characteristic changes caused by the chemical washing and painting process. Most important is the fact that the underside of the washed and painted rug is generally much lighter in color than the nap side. The underside is often a rose, even a very dull tannish rose on some rugs, while the nap will be plum or deep rose or deep red in color. Remember that the nap of a rug always fades to a lighter red rather than a darker tone. If the back of the rug is lighter than the pile side it is likely that the rug was bleached and then the nap redyed to a darker color. Next examine the nap to see if the edges of the design in blue or red are fuzzy, or if a little of the blue or red from the design has gone into the adjacent color. When the rug was redyed the worker many times did a slipshod job, spreading the dye into adjacent areas which should not have been colored.

These washed and painted Sarouks are the only rugs so treated that have lasted rather well. Some few will be in top condition (not having been used in areas of heavy traffic), but most will have begun to show some thinness and some will even have faded out spots in the red or rose field. A rug like this never becomes an antique and will be worth a fraction of the value of a good Sarouk. Finding Sarouks in a store at very high prices you might think the used painted Sarouk a good buy at half the price of a new rug. You would do better to figure the value of the washed rug at one-third the price--or less--of the new one.

FROM INDIA - Today a variety of rugs in traditional Sarouk designs are woven in nothern India (see Plates 6 and 7). Quality varies from average to superb, with the better grade Indian Sarouk an especially good value in today's market at one third the cost of an average quality Sarouk from Iran. New Iranian Sarouks can be bold and harsh in color; some of the Indian Sarouks are softer and more subtle in appearance and so blend more easily with traditional furnishings.

SARYK RUGS

From Russian Turkestan

One of the minor Turkoman tribal groups, Saryk rugs were woven at least as large as smaller carpet sizes. Often the color combination is darker and more somber than found in other Turkoman types with a deep, dull mahogany red common, sometimes with a purple cast. Saryk carpets often use a Tekke-like allover arrangement of "guls" or small medallions in the field, but the Saryk guls are often chunkier in proportion than the more familiar Tekke style, and somewhat bolder in effect. No old Saryk rugs are commonly available in commercial channels, but sometimes one does find new Afghan carpets of excellent quality in the Saryk design.

SAVONNEIRE RUGS

FROM FRANCE - Manufactures in 17th and 18th century France produced a wide variety of hand woven textiles including tapestries and pile rugs for the use of the nobles. The pile rugs were called Savonneries (after the name of a disused soap factory where production began). Most Savonneries came in large carpet sizes. Designs featured French floral patterns in soft shades of cream, rose, pale blue, wisteria, and muted green. Weave was rather coarse, but the pile was thick and heavy and of very good wool. Few if any antique French Savonneries would be available to a private buyer.

FROM OTHER EUROPEAN COUNTRIES - Interestingly enough there were at least a few pile Savonneries woven in Austria, Bulgaria, and Czechoslovakia as well as in France. A few of these European Savonneries came on the market in the 1930's among the thousands of rugs confiscated and sent abroad by the Russian government in an attempt to raise funds for development.

FROM INDIA - By far the most familiar source of rugs in Savonnerie design has been India. From 1946 to 1973 practically all the rugs woven in India were in two general designs, the French Savonnerie pattern and various Chinese motifs. Some seventy-five companies made Savonnerie rugs in lovely pastel shades (see Plate 26). They varied from very poor to very excellent quality. Years ago some cheap ones even had as much as 30% jute mixed with the carpet wool in their nap. Note: Every new rug imported to the United States must have a tag affixed indicating the material the rug is made of (100% wool pile, 70% wool and 30% jute, etc.)

Savonnerie rugs remain popular today for their formal design and soft pastel colors, but most Indian weavers prefer to make pieces in Iranian designs.

SENA RUGS
From Iran

No antique Senas have been imported since about 1930. Few new ones have been made in the past forty-five years. The antique Sena with silk warp was one of the most valuable rugs of the 19th century--a rare collector's item. The few Senas with cotton warp made since 1925 were for the most part mediocre rugs. They were not very finely woven nor were they choice or beautiful.

Designs in both older and newer Senas frequently made good use of the Herati motif. Fields may be red, blue, or ivory, but the intricate pattern made for a lively, attractive effect.

SENA-KELIM RUGS
From Iran

A flat stitch rug made by varying the colors of the warp threads in order to develop the design. The pattern is the same on both sides of the rug. The Sena-Kelim, although many types of kelims are made in the various rug weaving areas, was perhaps the choicest of them all. No new pieces have been available in years, and the supply coming from estates and individuals has declined as well.

SENA KURD RUGS
From Iran

In the past a variety of rug types from the Hamadan area were offered at wholesale and at retail as "Sena Kurds." Most dealers today would distinguish between these several varieties of Hamadan rugs which before were lumped together. Bibikabad, Ingelas, Borchalou, and Dergazine were the types most commonly offered as Sena Kurd. Some dealers made a simple distinction on the basis of quality, with better grade Hamadans offered as Sena Kurds.

SERAB RUGS
From Iran

Serab is the name of a village located southeast of the city of Herez in north-eastern Iran. Ninety percent of all the rugs made in the area before World War II were in runner sizes of 3 x 3½ ft. wide and lengths up to 18 ft. long, with most being 7 to 12 ft. in length. Designs almost always consisted of large repeated medallions in rust, rosey red, or blue. Accent colors of green, plum, gold, and red were common. Outer borders and central fields were often camel colored wool. Because Serab runners were often too wide for halls or stairways in American homes, it was the practice of some dealers to remove the outer border of a piece to make the runner fit the space. Although the name "Serapi" is taken from this village, there were no looms in Serab large enough to make carpet sized rugs until after World War II. Most "Serapis" were in fact woven in the vicinity of Herez. About 1960 some few 7 x 10 ft. Serabs appeared in the markets, but shortly afterward both runners and carpets became very scarce. There is still the chance of finding an old Serab runner from an estate, and if not given too heavy traffic the rug may well be in good condition even after 50 years' use.

SERAPI RUGS

FROM IRAN - No rugs have been imported by this name in the past 50 years; no carpets by this name can be traced to the village of Serab from which the name is taken. Rather, "Serapi" was a name devised by dealers for some rugs from the Herez district having certain characteristics of design and coloration, usually a pattern with more open ground and less allover design than other Herez and colors that run to soft terra cotta, ivory, and light blue. Actually there is considerable variety of design among the rugs woven in the different villages of the Herez district and the name Serapi has been applied somewhat inconsistently to carpets that seem to have been woven in separate villages.

In recent years use of the name Serapi has been revived. Many of the inquiries we receive come from the South, from people who see ads picturing "Serapi" rugs and seem to like the designs. The difficulty is that some dealers use the less familiar and more indefinite name Serapi for a common Herez in order to inflate the price of a particular rug in their stock. Remember that it is not just the name or age of a rug that makes it valuable. A very rare type will be worth comparatively little if it is very thin, worn, or heavily repaired. While dealers are free to offer old Herez rugs as "Serapis" we object to the idea of trying to upgrade old and for the most part worn out Gorevans, Mehribans, and other members of the Herez family in order to extract the maximum possible price from unsuspecting buyers.

FROM INDIA - Along with rugs in Herez design from India come pieces in "Serapi" motif and colors. Indian Serapis usually have geometric central medallion with stiffly angular leaf or vine elements filling the central field. Colors are often more muted than in Herez designs, with soft terra cotta, light blue or turquoise, green, navy, and gold as principal hues. Quality can vary a good deal from rug to rug, but such pieces are usually of medium weave with rather thick nap. They are much less costly than even an Iranian Herez.

SHIRAZ RUGS

FROM IRAN - Shiraz is a principal city in the Fars district of southern Iran. Over the years hundreds of rug types have come from Fars, most, for want of a more definite identification, simply called Shiraz. These rugs are the product of the nomadic and semi-nomadic peoples of the area. Most all Shiraz rugs have loose to medium weaves with wool warp and weft. Most have bold geometric designs and rusty red, blue, gold, and brown colors. Years ago many small mats and bag faces were available, as were scatter sizes and rugs up to about 7 x 10 ft. Because horizontal looms were used almost exclusively in the area, the maximum rug size that could be woven was limited.

Traditionally Shiraz rugs were rather inexpensive, although particularly fine or unusual peices were always more costly (as they are with any rug type). As the Reza Shah and his son settled the nomads and altered their way of life rug weaving declined along with the quality of individual rugs. The great oil development in southern Iran had its effect as well in limiting rug production and increasing labor costs. By the early 1970's many dealers had turned away from Shiraz for less expensive types. Among the last Shiraz-related types of good quality available was the Yalameh (see entry under "Yalameh").

FROM OTHER AREAS: Surprisingly enough there are some rugs woven in Rumania on woolen warp and weft in south Persian designs. These rugs in Transylvania quality compare very favorably with the typical Iranian Shiraz and are much less expensive. Dimensions are more varied as well, with 9 x 12 ft. and 10 x 14 ft. carpets sometimes available.

In the past decade some rugs in Shiraz designs have been woven in India. Destined mostly for the German market these pieces have all been on cotton warp and weft and so differ markedly in structure from Iranian Shiraz. Their major attraction has been their very inexpensive cost.

SHIRVAN RUGS

FROM THE CAUCASUS - Rugs of this type appeared most often in scatter sizes of 3½ x 5 ft. to 4½ x 7 ft. Weaves were usually fairly fine, and as a type Shirvans were always more closely clipped than some other Caucasian varieties. Almost all Shirvans had woolen warp and weft. A number of charateristic designs have been identified, but as with most other Caucasians patterns are always geometric, sometimes with pole medallion arrangement, sometimes with more allover motif.

An antique Shirvan in good condition is a valuable collector's item, although most of the old pieces will be at least slightly thin and many badly worn. No Shirvans from the Caucasus have been imported since well before World War II, and so supply is limited to those rugs from estates or collectors that may come on the market. Most Caucasian types are still avidly collected and so an old piece will be expensive.

FROM INDIA - There are good supplies of excellent rugs in Shirvan design woven in the Jaipur area of northern India. This district produces finely woven rugs of distinctive construction. A typical Jaipur district Shirvan will have 145 knots per square inch and a medium thick nap of very soft and lustrous wool. Most Jaipur area Shirvans are single wefted (that is, there is one weft shoot between adjacent rows of knots) and this construction results in a soft and fairly flexible carpet. Some Shirvans come in double wefted weave, and this weave makes for a stiffer foundation. Double wefted Shirvans sometimes have a thicker nap than single wefted rugs.

Designs are quite varied, with the "Akstafa star" pattern common (a series of star shaped medallions surrounded by geometric peacocks and other angular flower and vegetative forms--see Plate 11). Some Shirvans have perpedil-style allover designs, while some rugs even have patterns reminiscent of Iranian Ardebils and Mishkins.

Indian Shirvans are available in a wide variety of dimensions, from small mats (sometimes as small as 2 x 2 ft.) through runners and scatters and up through 9 x 12 ft., 10 x 14 ft., and sometimes even large carpets on the order of 12 x 18 ft.

FROM TURKEY - A variety of Turkish village rugs are found in Caucasian designs, and Shirvan motifs are well represented among them. Turkish weavers seem especially at home with the bold geometric figures of the old Shirvans, and the modern rugs they produce in the old designs can be very handsome (see Plates 20 and 21).

These pieces from India and Turkey are excellent values in today's market. Their fine quality and good wool make them natural replacements for the much more expensive and less available Caucasians. Indian and Turkish Shirvans can be used and enjoyed in a way the fragile old rug cannot.

SOUMAK RUGS

From Iran, Turkey, Central Asia, and the Caucasus

Soumak describes a flat weave, pile-less construction whereby the pattern of the rug is created by varying the color of the wefts as the weaving progresses. In Soumak construction, the weaver leaves a few inches of weft yarn loose at the back of the rug each time a new color is introduced. These strands of wool mat together to add thickness to the rug, providing the equivalent of a built-in carpet pad (unlike the Kelim, the Soumak is not reversible). Most Soumaks have simple geometric designs in reds, blues, browns, and greens.

SPARTA RUGS

From Turkey and Greece

Sparta rugs were produced in quantity in western Turkey and Greece up until the 1930's. They were first woven in Turkey, but the Turkish persecution of the Armenian community in Turkey caused many weavers to flee to Greece in 1915, where rug production was resumed by many of the immigrants.

Few varieties of Oriental rugs are less attractive than the Sparta. Even though handwoven, Spartas look like domestic or machine made rugs with clumsy floral designs and dyes and wool of mediocre quality. The identification of a rug as a Sparta should be taken as a warning to avoid it.

SUJ-BULAK RUGS

From Iran

No rugs or carpets have been imported by this name in the past 50 years and very infrequently will a rug of this type appear from an estate or elsewhere. The choice pieces woven up to about 1935 had very compact weave, woolen warp and weft, and Herati patterns reminiscent of some old Fereghans and Senas. Some Suj-Bulaks came in scatter sizes, but many came in long narrow carpet dimensions up to about 8 x 17 ft. Not a type likely to be encountered today.

SULTANABAD RUGS

From Iran

Sultanabad rugs from the vicinity of the city of Arak were plentiful and inexpensive in the period from 1948 through the late 1960's. Many of these were used and semi-antique rugs with softer colors than new rugs of the same type. Most of these rugs were in carpet sizes of about 10½ x 14 ft., but Sultanabads came in proportions from 7½ x 10½ ft. and 9 x 12 ft. up to as large as 12 x 14 ft. Most Sultanabads had allover floral designs including palmettes, blossoms, leaves, and vines on rusty red or rose-red ground. Some Sultanabads came with allover Feraghan design however, and Sultanabads with central medallions were common as well. Sometimes ivory or blue fields were found. Sultanabads were of average weave at best but their good wool made them fairly durable and their low cost and the availability of older rugs with softer colors made them a popular type.

Few if any Sultanabads have been imported in the past decade. As a type they simply lost out to the competition from India, Pakistan, and Rumania--to types which were of better quality but cost less.

TABRIZ

FROM IRAN - Over the past 150 years there have been many types, designs, and qualities of Tabriz rugs. Some of the Tabriz of the 19th century were rated among the choicest and finest of Persian rugs. Most were in carpet sizes and many employed a copper-colored open field. By 1928 this type was available in many qualities. During the Depression years prices dropped very low and there were still lovely old Tabriz in medium qualities available at reasonable prices up until about 1965.

TABA-TABAIE TABRIZ

In the early 1960's there appeared in the wholesale markets a new variety of Tabriz. These rugs were first woven by the Taba-Tabaie family, one of the famous rug making concerns of the city of Tabriz. These rugs were all in soft shades of rust, gold, green, blue, bittersweet, and beige. Patterns were taken from some of the most famous old museum rugs. Among the patterns most liked were 16th century animal and hunting designs, the garden design with a field divided into many small compartments, the 16th century Isphahan medallion design, and various vase and tree of life designs. Many of these rugs used the so-called "book design" with an open field enclosing a small medallion and elaborate inner border (see Plate 9). Some few of these new Tabriz came in geometric designs copying the old mosaic patterns found in the mosques of Tabriz.

These rugs quickly became the most popular Oriental type imported to the United States in 50 years. At least 75% of all Tabriz rugs made since 1960 were in the general designs and colors of this new type. Most of these rugs came to the New York market for which they were often specifically woven--the Germans do not favor these rugs (in the same way that they do not like the pastel ivory, light blue, and light rose colored Kirmans). They like bolder and stronger colors.

These Taba-Tabaie Tabriz took America by storm. Sizes ranged from small mats through 6 x 9 ft., 9 x 12 ft., and much larger carpets. These Tabriz quickly made inroads on the sale of Kirmans throughout the country, though many Kirman owners still favored the Kirman. There was never an Oriental type from Iran which appealed to so many of our customers. This was especially true of rugs in carpet sizes--6 x 9 ft., 8 x 10 ft., 9 x 12 ft., and larger sizes. These pieces had antique designs and colors soft enough to go easily with antique rugs. The average Persian rug of the past 50 years had been too bright and colorful for many decors. This is the reason why so many types of Persian carpets were treated chemically to soften their colors.

The real Taba-Tabaie Tabriz was as a rule the least bit more finely woven than most of the other new Tabriz but some others were of similar quality and just as expensive. They are woven in many small sizes to large scatter rugs, and in many runner sizes, as well as in all the carpet sizes. Beginning in the late 1960's the prices for Tabriz rugs rose sharply. At the same time, in the rush to turn out more rugs and to hold prices down, the quality of some Tabriz rugs was lowered. Tabriz rugs can vary a great deal in quality, and today the best have priced themselves out of the market except for very well-to-do buyers.

Sales of Iranian Tabriz have suffered badly from competition with Indian and Rumanian rugs in Tabriz design. Iranian Tabriz remain available in limited numbers in today's market but at such high prices that few will be sold.

FROM INDIA - A variety of large carpets in Tabriz designs were woven in India in the 1920's and 1930's. In the last several years the supply of Tabriz from India has exploded, providing an unwelcome shock to the Iranian weavers of the Tabriz district. Tabriz rugs from India are available in all the classic designs, hunting, garden, tree of life, medallion, book, etc., and in a wide range of qualities. Indian Tabriz rugs of the best grades are superior to the Taba-Tabaie rugs of the late 1960's and yet are one-third to one-half the price. Good Indian Tabriz are difficult for the average rug customer to differentiate from Iranian Tabriz except on the basis of price.

TAFRISH RUGS
From Iran

These Hamadan-like rugs come from a weaving district about 50 miles from Hamadan. All came in sizes of approximately 4½ x 6 ft., and all came in the same general design, a central medallion pattern with relatively curvilinear floral motif. Colors were normally a rose or rosey lavender field with medallion in blue or salmon, corners in ivory, and borders in ivory or light blue. Many more Tafrish seem to have gone to Europe than came to the United States, although a few will be found among the used and semi-antique Hamadans that come from tag sales or in trade to dealers.

TAI MING RUGS
From Taiwan

A good quality Chinese rug brought to the United States after World War II in small numbers. By 1973 prices had risen to the point where the major importer of this type discontinued his orders. An older Tai Ming is virtually indistinguishable from a carved Chinese of 70 or 90 line quality woven in mainland China during the same period.

TAI PING OR TAI PEI RUGS
Hand tufted in Hong Kong

These are not real Oriental rugs but rather hand tufted rugs. They do not have the individually hand-tied knots that are used in constructing a genuine Oriental. Instead the rug is tufted on a manufactured backing in the same way a hooked rug is produced. Large strands of wool are used, with as few as 9 to 16 wool strands to the square inch. The nap usually has some hand carving. The back of the rug is usually latexed to hold in the wool tufts and then covered with a muslin scrim. Since these are not Oriental rugs their resale value is low. There is the danger that some buyers have been misled into believing they were purchasing a genuine Oriental when they selected one of these tufted rugs.

TALISH RUGS
From the Caucasus

A rare type of old Caucasian rug. Always in the same general design with an open plain field in either blue or red, and almost invariably with border design of small rosettes on an ivory background. The narrow guard borders usually have small geometric blossoms. Seeing one you should easily recognize another of this type. Not finely woven--the weave is usually between that of a Shirvan and a Kazak in knot count. None imported in fifty years. There is a chance that eventually some new rugs in this design may come out of Russia.

TEKKE RUGS
From Russian Turkestan

Old Tekke rugs from Russian Turkestan are today available only from estates or among the old rugs dealers may purchase or take in trade. The Tekkes were the most numerous of the Turkoman peoples in the 19th century, and of the surviving Turkoman weavings of this period most are of Tekke manufacture. Old Tekke bags, scatter rugs, and carpets were often very tightly woven, and most were closely clipped rugs woven on woolen warp and weft. Colors are almost always red (although the red can vary from rosey red through wine, liver red, or even a plum or mahogany red), and designs typically use the small octagonal medallion shape or "gul" that is so associated with Tekke weaving.

When the power of the Tekkes was broken by the might of the Russian army at Geok Tepe in 1881 Turkoman culture began a long decline. Numbers of Tekkes and other Turkoman peoples moved from Russian Turkestan into adjacent areas that today form parts of Iran and Afghanistan. Designs went with them, and so today there are rugs in Tekke or Tekke-derived designs woven in southern Russia, northern Iran, Afghanistan, Pakistan, and northern India. The quality and cost of these rugs can differ tremendously.

For years the tightly woven thickly napped Karachi grade Bokharas in Tekke design from Pakistan have been especially good values. These beautiful rugs in old Tekke design have the muted but rich colors that go so well with traditional furnishings. Other grades besides the Karachi type are available in Tekke design, with some of the finest rivaling the old Turkoman rugs for quality of workmanship (see the entry under "Bokhara" for more information about rugs of Turkoman type).

TRICLINIUM RUGS

Before World War II there occasionally appeared large carpets from Iran that were woven to look as though four rugs had been combined. If the whole carpet was 16 x 22 ft., for instance, one end of the rug would be woven to look like a runner, complete with separate borders and field that was oriented to run across the end of the rug. This area would measure about 5 x 16 ft. Both sides of the carpet would be woven to look like matching runners that measured about 3 x 17 ft. each. The remaining central area of the rug would have its own border and field design, and would measure about 10 x 17 ft. in size. At one time there seem to have been sets of matching rugs in the above dimensions woven for use in the central room of an Iranian home, and the Triclinium carpets seem to be a latter development whereby the look of the four separate rugs was combined into one carpet. It would be unusual to find an intact Triclinium today.

TURKBAFF RUGS
From Iran

No new Turkbaff rugs (literally "Turkish knot" rugs) have been imported commercially in a decade. These pieces were all in carpet sizes and were the choicest of the types woven in Meshed and the Khurasan district. Many rugs were imported as Turkbaffs and then advertised and sold as Isphahans. We called some of these "Isphahan Meshed" to distinguish them from Meshed rugs which were of much lesser quality.

Most Turkbaffs were tightly woven rugs on cotton foundation with medium thick to thick naps. Designs were many and varied, almost always floral patterns although some Feraghan designs came as well.

While a buyer will not find a selection of new Turkbaff rugs, an old one might appear. There are a variety of excellent new carpets from India in colors and designs and of a quality very reminiscent of the old Turkbaffs.

TZI TZI RUGS
From the Caucasus

A common German spelling for "Chi-Chi" (see entry under "Chi Chi" for notes about this rare Caucasian type).

VASE CARPETS
From Iran

For want of a better name a group of antique Iranian carpets are usually classed together as "vase carpets." As the name suggests, the design of these rugs usually is a balanced arrangement of vases with floral display. Weave is especially tight and the pattern very intricate. Animal and bird figures are rarely present. Most of these pieces are in larger dimensions and they are obviously the product of a court-sponsored workshop. Two large "vase carpets" flank the world famous Ardebil Mosque carpet in the Victoria and Albert Museum in London, while the Metropolitan Museum in New York has an excellent example of the type presented by B. Altman around 1920.

Over the years rugs from many weaving areas have used this vase motif: Kirman, Tabriz, Qum, Kashan, and other types have all appeared in the pattern. It is not surprising that rugs in this design were always more popular in Europe than in America.

VERAMIN RUGS
From Iran

None have been imported since about 1935. These rugs were made by Kurdish weavers in the area of Veramin, a town a short distance southeast of Tehran. Many appeared as pillows approximately 15 to 20 inches wide by 2½ x 3 ft. long. Most had rich navy blue background with allover "Mina Khani" design. Many of these rugs were sold as Bahktiari. With wool foundation and excellent workmanship and design these small rugs were always of interest to hobbyists and collectors. Not many pieces of this type will be found today.

YALAMEH RUGS
From Iran

This fairly new rug type from southern Iran began to appear in the markets in the early 1960's. Most Yalamehs are woven in the vicinity of the city of Abedeh by once nomadic peoples now transformed into farmers and villagers by the policies of the Shah. Many characteristics link Yalameh as a type with the nomadic rugs produced in the area in previous years.

As a type Yalameh rugs usually have medium weave (although tighter than most Shiraz) and warps and wefts of wool. Yalamehs are usually thick rugs and the quality of wool is often excellent. A typical design employs a series of connected medallions fringed with latchhooks with angular flowers, leaves, and vines as the border treatment. Some Yalamehs have a pattern of large rhomboids linked into an allover design, but features are always strongly geometric. Colors often include red, camel, blue, and a good deal of green (see Plate 2). Most production of these rugs is in 2 x 3 ft. mats and 3½ x 5 ft. scatters. A limited number of runners and carpets in the 8 x 10 ft. and 9 x 12 ft. sizes appeared in the mid 1970's but these sizes are less common now.

In the recent past Yalamehs have lost ground because of their higher prices to the good Turkish village rugs, but they are an interesting variety. If the economy of Iran can be stabilized so that trade and export revive, rug types like Yalameh may again become available.

YEZD RUGS
From Iran

A rare variety since none are imported and few were ever brought to America. The type came from the area around Yezd northwest of Kirman. All were in carpet sizes with most larger than 9 x 12 ft. Quality varied, with the best about the same in weave as a medium grade Kirman or Tabriz. Nap was medium to medium-short, and patterns were often central medallion with open field in cochineal red or magenta with accents of blue, ivory, pink, and green. Not a type that was ever particularly popular in America or that was of commercial importance.

YOMUD RUGS
From Russian Turkestan

One of the Turkoman tribal types, Yomud rugs have not been available in any quantity in recent years. Up until World War II many tent bags (rugs with a handwoven Kelim backing opening on the long side to form a carrying bag) could be found in the London market. These bags were the suitcase or trunk in which the Yomud carried everything from clothes to kitchen utensils. Smaller bags of about 12 x 18 inches to 2 x 5 ft. were also made. Some rugs came as small as the 6 x 4 ft. size, but most were about 5 x 9 ft. through 6 x 12 ft. All features were geometric and colors almost invariably in a mahogany or brownish wine. Few larger rugs have been available in forty years' time. Few if any new rugs from Russia or Afghanistan come in these designs but a few Pakistani rugs are occasionally found with Yomud motif.

YURUK RUGS
From Turkey

In his COMPLETE GUIDE Colonel Jacobsen noted that no new Yuruk rugs had been made since about 1915. In fact while old pieces are rarely found in today's markets, some new rugs in Yuruk design are again available from Turkey.

Made in western Turkey Yuruk rugs (the name means "nomad") are usually of moderate weave with fairly thick nap of excellent wool. All of the recent examples we have seen were woven in the old style on woolen warp and weft. Colors often include magenta red with accents of ivory, green, salmon, and plum. Features are virtually always geometric or abstractly floral, and prayer rugs are not uncommon. Most new Yuruks will be found in 3 x 4½ ft., 4½ x 6 ft., and 5 x 7 ft. sizes.

ZELI-SULTAN RUGS
From Iran

These pieces came invariably in a size of about 4 x 6 ft. and the majority were in an easily recognized pattern, an allover flower filled vase design, but some came with a Feraghan design as well. Old pieces were tightly knotted with closely clipped nap. In the 1920's and 1930's the type was avidly collected, even though some examples had a loose red that was apt to bleed into adjacent colors.

There was always some doubt as to just where these pieces were made. The Hamadan district has been advanced as a source, but it is the case that rugs in the Zeli-Sultan design have been found from Qum as well. In the 1960's some Abadeh rugs from southern Iran used this design, most often on ivory ground.

PART III

CHAPTER ELEVEN

ANTIQUE ORIENTAL RUGS

Rare antique Oriental rugs are ranked with great paintings, sculpture, and musical compositions as great art. One needs no proof to substantiate the fact that choice antique rugs are considered one of the highest forms of art. Museums the world over have exhibited their beauty. Some of the wealthiest individuals in America and abroad have spent millions in collecting rare antique Oriental rugs.

HOW OLD IS AN ANTIQUE RUG? Most authorities agree in the opinion that a rug must be fifty years old to be called "antique." Others will insist that for the rug to be a real antique it must have been woven before 1875, and that the fifty year old rug might be called a "semi-antique" or a "practical antique." Very few rugs are dated and even if they are there are frequently problems in interpreting precisely what the date on the rug represents according to the western calendar. Mr. Arthur Upham Pope of the Art Institute of Chicago says, in discussing what might be called an antique rug, "Ignoring dates we can say that an antique rug is one that has not been chemically washed, that has an unrestored pile, and was woven according to local methods before the latter was extensively modified by European influence."

BUT ANTIQUE DOES NOT MAKE A RUG CHOICE, RARE OR VALUABLE.
There are many average and even poor rugs woven before 1900 (as there are choice and unusual rugs woven in this century) and these rugs even when old are seldom valuable. But the chances are that the old rug in good condition is more than likely a good rug simply because the poorer ones will have worn out sooner. In this instance, good wool quality will have been the reason for the rug's condition and beauty and classification as a collector's item.

Good wool is the most important factor in giving the rug long life, in making it more beautiful as times passes, and in determining whether it is just an Oriental rug representative of its type or in fact a rare rug. Good wool means that the rug will have developed a lovely natural patina and sheen as it ages. Two rugs of the same name with the same general design and made at the same time may very well differ greatly as to value after fifty years. The one with superior wool will be in much better condition, much more beautiful, and worth ten times more than the one made with rather poor or dry wool.

AN ORIENTAL RUG HAS THREE VALUES
The value of an antique Oriental rug has three components: the utility value, the art value, and the collector's value. The utility value depends upon the durability of the rug as a floor covering. The art value depends upon the design and colors of the rug rather than the texture and fineness of weave (even though fineness is desirable in most types of rugs). The collector's value depends upon the rarity of the rug in question plus the art value, and especially upon the rug's being one of the choicest and one of the most beautiful of its type. Fineness of weave does not necessarily, by itself, make a rug a collector's item. For example, many of the coarser antique Turkish rugs are perhaps more valuable than some of the finer Persian rugs of the same period. This is also true of many rare old Caucasian rugs less finely woven than many antique Persians.

CONDITION IS IMPORTANT IN AN ANTIQUE RUG

The better the condition of an antique rug the more valuable is the rug. A thin antique rug has some value. One that is completely worn out, that is threadbare, or that shows large areas of warp and weft has little or no value. Even a rare rug that is worn threadbare has very little value unless the specimen is nearly extinct. It is disturbing, even shocking, to find antique dealers and even some rug dealers pricing ordinary dilapidated rugs at ridiculously high prices when they are in fact nearly worthless. In some cases these "rare antiques" belong nowhere else but in the trash bin.

ANTIQUES ARE SCARCE

Antique rugs are seldom available in numbers today. No antique rugs of any note have been imported to America in the last twenty years. Very few semi-antique rugs have been imported into this country in the last fifteen years. Antique rugs are not even available in the weaving countries. They hardly exist in any numbers in Iran or elsewhere. Some few are in the homes and tents, mosques and palaces of old Iran, but the general statement that they do exist in the Orient is true. Some European dealers have accumulated stocks bought in America twenty years ago and are asking fantastic prices for the rugs they hold-- prices far beyond their true worth.

It is the sad fact that German and other European dealers have stripped America of most good antiques during the last three decades. With Germany emerging as a country of wealth with a hunger and appreciation for Oriental rugs, German buyers swarmed throughout America in the years from about 1955 to 1970. They bought thousands of antique rugs from small antique dealers in New York City and from retail dealers all over America. We have long refused to sell antique rugs to be exported. Up until a few years ago seldom a day passed but one or more German dealers appeared in our store. New York jobbers or antique dealers are still traveling about trying to outwit the local retail dealer into selling his antique rugs to them. These jobbers, in turn, make a handsome profit from European dealers or some antique collectors.

BEWARE OF AUCTIONS

Be wary in buying antique Oriental rugs at established auctions, let alone from an itinerant auctioneer. One is not going to find a good antique at the traveling auction at any price. Anyone who buys there in competition with shills (the auctioneer's employees whose job it is to bid the price up) deserves his fate. Of course, auctions like these are not true auctions as at most of these sales the auctioneers will not sell even to the highest bidder unless the price reaches a certain minimum level predetermined by the autioneer himself.

Not even at private estate sales are you safe. You may think that at a well advertised auction of a private estate you will buy an antique rug at a good price. The risk here is that the layman will see dealers bidding at big prices for a few rare rugs and that he who happens not to be knowledgeable about rugs will bid high for a rug worth very little. We recently saw a worn-out Balouchi bid at and sold for $220 when the actual value of the rug was about $15. Cases like this are all too common.

Collector rugs only seldom come from private homes. A "collection" is not just an assortment of rugs. To be a collector's item the rug must be a superb example of its type, not just any antique rug in any condition. The rug does not have to be a finely woven piece, but it must be one of the best of its type. Here is a list of rugs of which every collector would like to own an example: from Turkey we have the Ghiordes, Kula, Ladik, Bergamo, Melez, Hereke, Mudjar, Konia, Makri; from Persia the types that are perhaps most sought after are Bijar, Feraghan, Laver Kirman, Sena, Joshigan, Tabriz, Sarouk, Shiraz, Sujbulak; from Caucasia there are the wonderful old examples in Kuba, Karabagh, Chi-Chi, Baku, Kazak, and Gendje weave. From Central Asia the Tekke, Salor, Pinde, Yomud, and Beshire are most in demand. But search as you will among scores of dealers, you will be lucky to come up with even a few of these types. Any superb rug, even in the coarsest weave, is a collector's item.

Finally, a person of moderate circumstances should not and cannot hope to find rare rugs in prime condition for little money. Unless the seeker of antique rugs is simply set on antiques and nothing else he will do well to consider some of the lovely choice new rugs in traditional antique designs that are available today. Many of these have refined colors which would go with antiques and will undoubtedly be better property ten or twenty years from now than the worn, thin old rug. Such types as Nain, Isphahan, Yalameh, Abadeh, Bijar, Qum, some of the Bokharas from Pakistan, some of the village rugs from Turkey, as well as rugs from Pakistan and Afghanistan are available and worthy of consideration. Not all of these will go with antiques, but with a little careful screening one will find rugs as pretty as the most beautiful antiques, rugs that will go well with old furnishing and that will have lasting value.

CHAPTER TWELVE

AUCTIONS

The itinerant auctioneer of Oriental rugs is fast becoming discredited all over the country. Only the most gullible will buy a rug from the itinerant auctioneer. It is clear that the disreputable itinerant auctioneer of Oriental rugs could not survive one day without the illegal practice of using "shills" to raise bids on the rugs offered to a predetermined level, and to bid them in when they do not reach the price level required.

These auctions have seldom been a success in areas where there are reliable Oriental rug stores. They exist only in outlying towns and small cities where there are no nearby rug dealers. The people running the auctions are notorious for exaggerating the merits and the value of the rugs they offer. At a recent auction we monitored, for example, the auctioneer stated that a particular rug was worth $475 at retail. This small Indian rug was actually worth about $50 and would sell for this amount at a reputable rug store. Frequently the rugs offered by the traveling auctioneer are actually the rejects and leftovers from the wholesale markets. Some medium quality rugs may be included in the auctioneer's stock. In comparison to the many poor rugs these look much better than they really are and so can be sold at inflated prices.

In practically every one of the scores of articles about Oriental rugs that have appeared in the last few years the public has been warned against buying Oriental rugs from the itinerant auctioneer. Typical is an article about Oriental rugs in BARRON'S MAGAZINE: [1] " . . . . it is advisable to stay away from traveling auctioneers . . . . Your safest bet is a reputable dealer or department store with long experience in Oriental rugs. They will let you try an Oriental rug in your own home for a trial period." Another informative article about Oriental rugs and auctions appeared in the PHILADELPHIA ENQUIRER: [2] "Whenever large numbers of persons begin waving around large numbers of dollars for a commodity they don't know much about, the con men can't be far behind. It's happening in art, it's always affected antique prices, and now that Oriental rugs have replaced knee deep, wall-to-wall carpeting in interior decoration for those who seek status, the chances of being bilked are greater than ever." The article contains this example:
"There was the suburban Philadelphia woman who was unhappy with the looks of her roomsized Bokhara rug when she got it home. So she dragged it back to the itinerant rug auction where she had purchased it, expecting the money-back, unconditional refund she was promised, both verbally and in brochures. After a lengthy dispute, she realized that the men who ran the auction had no intention of giving a refund and there was nothing she could do about it outside a courtroom." The article characterizes most rug auctions this way:
"Although misidentifying one of the hundreds of styles of rugs, or misjudging age and quality, or paying more than a rug is worth is easy (even for experts) under many circumstances, it is at the itinerant auction where the consumer is in the biggest danger of being taken on a magic carpet ride. These auctions are run by dealers who are generally based in New York City where they buy both new and used rugs from jobbers. They travel into cities around the country, setting up sales in suburban motels and hotels and advertising prices 'lower than local retailers.' Or they offer special collections of unique and fine--even museum quality--rugs at bargain prices and an entertaining afternoon or evening at an

---

[1] James Powell, "Flying Carpets," Barron's Magazine, 16 Aug. 1976.
[2] Carroll Stoner, "Floating Sales Can Take You for a Carpet Ride," Philadelphia Enquirer, 10 Apr. 1975.

auction. But only rarely do they deliver on their promises. Price comparisons show that their advertised 'guaranteed lower than retail prices' are, in fact, almost always higher."

As Mr. Bernard Hart, head of the National Auction Association notes, "These are not auctions at all since real auctions generally deal in articles the auction house or auctioneer holds on consignment, not their own goods. This type of auction plucks ficticious bids out of the air and plants the audience with its own people who push the bids up. Shenanigans like this make me angry and make all auctions suspect."

Reputable rug dealers can help the public by bringing legal pressures to bear on the itinerant auctioneer. The auctioneer should be able to furnish an inventory of his stock and should be willing to post a bond against sales taxes that may be due on the rugs he sells. It is common knowledge that most itinerant auctions are not true auctions at all since many bids are made by shills, undercover representatives of those who are selling the rugs. If the rugs are not bid up to prices which the owners are trying to obtain, the shill makes a bid and appears outwardly to have bought the rug when in fact there was no sale and the rug is still owned by the original party. It is known that when one of these sham auctions is conducted, only a small fraction of the rugs which appear to be sold are actually paid for. Many of the "sold" rugs, in fact, are put back on the truck which then moves on to another city where the same performance takes place. In almost all localities it is an illegal act to conduct a mock auction where it is pretended that merchandise is sold when in fact it is not.

CHAPTER THIRTEEN

ORIENTAL RUGS AS INVESTMENT

There have appeared hundreds of articles in newspapers and magazines over the years glorifying Oriental rugs as great investments and indicating that Oriental rugs should be bought with the idea that they will increase in value. "GOOD RUG LIKE GOLD - Importer says." That was the headline of a recent article in the Macon, Georgia TELEGRAPH written about a New York importer who was holding a sale there. The article states that, "Currently Oriental rugs have better appreciation rates than real estate or even South African gold." A very well known store in New York used this banner in their ad in the NEW YORK TIMES: "EVERY RUG A SUPERB INVESTMENT."

Certainly articles and ads like these have helped the Oriental rug business. No doubt they have helped our company as well as others. Then you ask, what is your objection to saying Oriental rugs are a good investment? Giving the impression that any and all Oriental rugs are an investment in the sense that they will be worth much more in time and that they will yield a capital gain is wrong. This is cheap talk and at best is only partially true. A good Oriental rug bought at an honest price has proven to be a good investment and will no doubt prove to be one in the future, but certainly not all Orientals have this potential.

First, what is a good Oriental rug? What is a fair and honest price? What Oriental rugs sold in the past fifty years have proved to be investments? What rugs bought today are likely to increase in value? Nearly all Iranian rugs bought up until about 1973 would cost far more to replace than they did when purchased simply because the sharp rise in the price of rugs from Iran has come since 1972. Inflation and oil riches, child labor laws and the industrialization of Iran resulted in sharply higher prices for even inferior rugs. So, most of the new Iranian rugs bought in the last twenty-five years have increased sharply in price, and especially so since 1973.

Of course, rug types that were bad buys years ago have not proven to be good property. One thinks especially of the hundreds of used Chinese rugs which were sold at used rug sales at very high prices over the years. These rugs will seldom bring half their original price when they are sold today.

It seems more ethical and accurate to tell the customer that Oriental rugs are the most beautiful of all rugs, that they are the most economical of all rugs in that they usually will last a lifetime or longer, and that good rugs generally have some real resale value when you no longer need them. What more can you ask of a furnishing that is walked on for years? In this sense an Oriental is a "good investment," but it is not an investment in the same way that one can so describe stocks and bonds. Unfortunately this is exactly the impression that so many articles have created.

A good Oriental does not have to be a very rare antique in good condition, or even one of the finest woven of new rugs. Actually most antique rugs will be thin or worn. Such rugs if used on the floor will decline in value as their condition worsens. Certainly no chemically washed and painted rug will be a good investment since this is one type of rug that can never be classified antique or semi-antique but simply "used." A good rug should be one in good condition and a rug not chemically treated; also we probably would add, a rug in traditional design.

The dealers who proclaim any Oriental rug to be an investment forget the fact that two-thirds of all Oriental rugs sold in the period from 1920 - 1960 were both chemically washed and painted. The poor ones from this period have been thrown away as worn out. Even most of the once plentiful Lillihans are not still in use. Most Lillihans, had they been natural colored and not injured with chemicals and not painted, would be in good condition and would be worth much more than what was paid for them.

The Oriental rugs that have increased most in value are those antiques assembled by collectors up until about 1950. Many of these have become very valuable and scarce. Collectors generally will have selected their purchases carefully and will have taken good care of their rugs. Most of these rugs are types now very difficult to find, rugs that come on the market only from estates and types that rug enthusiasts have written about in such glorious terms. It is rugs like these that are responsible for the impression that any Oriental rug is a good investment.

If we talk only about the rugs bought in the last thirty-five to forty years the talk of great increases is true. But one must also look where the dollar has gone in that time–it is perhaps worth only 25% as much as it was thirty-five years ago. Of course if the customer overpays for a rug it has less chance of becoming more valuable, at least in the near future. There are many gullible people who think that the more they pay the better the rug, and in the Oriental rug business there unfortunately are many operators (especially the itinerant auctioneer) who are ready to extract the maximum price.

WHAT RUGS SOLD TODAY ARE MOST LIKELY TO INCRASE IN VALUE?

Colonel Jacobsen has his opinions. In his view the Karachi quality (9 x 18 double) Bokhara is one of the best values available today. These rugs have the potential for good future increase. For those who like the thinner and slightly finer rugs, the fine Bokharas made for Europe are good bets although for floor use the thicker 9 x 18 double is more durable. Any Iranian rug of a quality equal to these Bokharas would cost twice as much.

Also the best quality rugs from Pakistan in Persian designs like Kashan, Sarouk, Isphahan, and Tabriz are superior rugs sure to be valuable property in years to come. It is difficult for the layman to tell whether these rugs are made in Iran or Pakistan. Since they cost so much less than the equivalent Iranian types they would seem to be excellent values. Many of these rugs are actually better than their Iranian counterparts in materials and workmanship.

The excellent Persian design rugs coming from India will also prove to be good property. The best of the rugs produced there are great values, available for less money than the lower grades of Iranian rugs. Indian production continues to improve and their prices at present are less than half those of Iranian types of equivalent quality.

There is some fear that the West Germans and other buyers will send the prices of all these rugs from India and other weaving countries up sharply. That has happened in India in the past, and for twenty years the demand for rugs from Germany has upped prices in Iran. Never forget that the Germans stripped America of many thousands of her choicest antique Orientals by their willingness to pay dearly for the rugs they wanted. They are partially responsible for the very high prices of antique Oriental rugs in the United States.

CHAPTER FOURTEEN

CHEMICAL WASHING AND PAINTING OF ORIENTAL RUGS

There is no more washing and painting of Oriental rugs. This despicable--but once popular--process of chemically bleaching and retouching Oriental rugs came to an end about 1960. The treatment was done after the rugs reached America. Colonel Jacobsen covered the details of this process thoroughly in his COMPLETE GUIDE. The process began about 1905 as the stocks of older rugs available in Iran began to run out. Dealers were afraid buyers would shun bright new rugs, and developed ways of making new rugs look old. The idea was to soften the bright colors in order to make the rugs more saleable.

Today some of the better washed and painted Sarouks coming from estates that were sold during the Depression years are being bought up by jobbers who in turn make a good profit from the sale of these washed and painted rugs to the Germans and Italians. Some few of these Sarouks are in good condition after 50 years, others are slightly worn to worn thin. The thousands of Hamadans, Kirmans, Lillihans, and others so treated and sold during the 1920's and 1930's are worn out by now, unless they happened to have unusually light use. These rugs never became semi-antique or antique, but generally decreased in value steadily.

Many rugs received both the chemical washing and painting process, but there were also less harmful methods of softening the colors in a rug. One method is to wash the rug with a mild lime solution or light chlorine solution. Almost all of the Kirmans have always had this light treatment. When the painting process became so expensive, most of the Sarouks were given a light wash instead of the heavy chemical stripping they received before. All of the thousands and thousands of Chinese rugs that were imported in the 1920's were given a light chemical washing. They were crude and unsaleable without it. All the earlier authors and authorities approved of this light washing. It did not seem to affect to any extent the wearing qualities of the rugs so treated.

In Iran was developed what we called the Persian wash--a very light treatment to tone down the colors of new rugs. We frankly liked it and it did little or no harm to the durability of the rug. It cost very little in Iran. The light treatment done in Pakistan and in India seems to have little effect on wear either. The wash does add luster to the rug.

CHAPTER FIFTEEN

JUFTI KNOTS AND DYES

JUFTI KNOTS - In simple words, when the weaver ties a Jufti knot he ties the knot on four warp strings instead of the usual two. The result is that the rug has half the density of wool pile it would otherwise have. But few rugs (except for some rugs from the Khorassan district) ever used more than about 10% Jufti knots. The use of a few Juftis did not materially affect the quality or the durability of the rug. It did mean a 10% increase in pay for the weaver in view of the weaving time and cost of the wool saved.

Only in the Eastern province of Iran in the Khorassan district has the Jufti knot been used for generations in weaving the entire rug. In fact the practice was restricted mostly to the Hamadan and Khorassan districts of Iran. In Hamadan, weavers sometimes used the Jufti knot in order to hold prices down by using less time and less wool. One was sure that some of the Bibikabad carpets and Hosseinabads used some Jufti knots but even in their coarser weaves with fewer knots they were very durable rugs. Jufti knots occasionally appear in rugs from India, Pakistan, and Turkey as well but rarely are they so numerous in these rugs as to affect the value of the carpet. The question of Jufti knots should not be of great concern to the rug buyer. It would take an expert and a detailed study of a rug to detect the 10% Jufti knots that might be present.

DYES - No doubt we will shock some of the collectors and students of Oriental rugs when we advise the prospective buyer of a new rug to forget the question of vegetable vs. synthetic dyes and to rely instead upon the dealer or store from whom you buy your rug to be responsible for the integrity of dyes in the rug. If you buy a rug and later when it is cleaned the colors run and stain adjacent light colored areas the reliability of the dealer is your only recourse. If the colors fade badly in a very short time under normal use and the rug loses its beauty, the dealer should certainly make a satisfactory adjustment (the chances of this kind of fading are so remote that perhaps it should not even be considered). Certainly you want the colors in your rug to mellow a bit with time. That is why a semi-antique, antique, or used rug is often preferred to a new rug of the same type. We would gladly change a customer's older rug with softened colors for a new rug of the same type if the customer wanted to retain the brighter tones. You want the ivory to tone to cream, the bright greens, blues, and reds to mellow. The Iranian rug with ten year's use is generally more saleable than a colorful new rug.

The whole controversy about vegetable dyes vs. synthetic dyes began in the early rug books written by Mumford, Hawley, and Lewis (published between 1900 and 1913). These were the three standard books in the libraries and the main references for buyers and collectors. When our business began in 1924 the question most asked was about dyes. Even in 1924 there was no real issue because not one rug out of a thousand that came to America had loose or faded colors and most all of these rugs used synthetic dyes. For all these years a more immediate evil has been the chemical washing and painting of rugs after they arrived in America.

Why do we advise that a buyer forget the question of vegetable vs. synthetic dyes? Principally because few if any retail dealers, any importers, or even most of the small dealers in Iran or other countries can tell you what the chemical composition is of most of the dyes in the rugs that pass through their hands. The big producer in India or China, of course, knows the origin of the dyes for the different colors he furnished to the weavers. In Iran a few of the colors in one rug will be vegetable dyes, some perhaps aniline and most chromium synthetic dyes. City rugs probably used synthetic dyes first and tribal rugs last, but without the help of an analytical chemist it is not possible to know the composition of the dyestuff in a particular rug for sure. It is generally accepted that synthetic dyes were widely available in Persia, Turkey, and the Caucasus in the 1880's and that wherever and as soon as available they were preferred by weavers over the "vegetable" alternatives. The first aniline dyes were clearly unsatisfactory for coloring wool, and it was these early aniline dyes that gave synthetic colors such a bad reputation. By World War I, however, there were few rug types still made which used totally vegetable colors. Chrome dyes were specifically created for use with organic fibers and these synthetics were used for all colors except for those shades for which a very plentiful and inexpensive local source existed.

If you examine a rug and find badly run color you should question the dealer and probably avoid the rug. If your new rug is washed properly and the colors run the dealer from whom you bought it should make proper adjustment. Sometimes a rug will be washed successfully several times and then betray loose colors. Color run in such a case is almost always due to the use of an inappropriate detergent or soap or to the use of hot water instead of tepid water in the wash.

CHAPTER SIXTEEN

CARE OF RUGS

Information about the care of rugs is widely available. Most is simple common sense: try to keep the rug clean, protect it from unusual conditions like tracked in salt or repeated drenching wetness, mothproof the rug occasionally or if it will be stored unused, and promptly repair worn areas of the fringe or edge bindings.

Among general recommendations we suggest you do not send your rugs out to be professionally cleaned more often than really necessary. If you examine the pile of your rug carefully and note an accumulation of dirt and grit deep down in the nap the rug should be cleaned professionally. However, to routinely send your rug out to be "professionally" cleaned every year or two can in fact do more harm than good. Some rug cleaners are "professionals" only in the sense that they will take money for what they do. Many use a rotating scrubbing machine to shampoo the rug but do not have a means to thoroughly rinse the rug. No great harm may be done by one or two washings like this if a gentle oil base soap is used, but the cumulative effect of frequent washings of this kind can be dramatic. A scrubbing machine with a stiff brush can take off some of the nap of the rug in just one cleaning (if the brush is first soaked so that the bristles are made soft and pliable most of the chance for damage is removed). To be thoroughly cleaned the rug should be saturated so that all the soap is rinsed out with lots of water. Inquire about the cleaner in your area, go see his plant and his equipment and method and ask questions. Inquire of some friends who have used a cleaner's services for a good many years. You can often do a pretty good job yourself once a year or oftener with a soft brush, a pail of cool water, and any good soap.

"STEAM" CLEANING MACHINE - This process does not really use steam but rather water with an applicator and vacuum extractor. These machines are often available for rent. We are not yet prepared to recommend or disapprove of this process. This process works well when used in homes on wall-to-wall carpeting and on large pastel Orientals from India. It seems to be good for these and to do no harm. We would prefer to wash the rug by hand with a gentle soap and then use the machine with clean water to rinse the rug. If a good cleaner is available in your area we would still prefer to send out a very dirty rug to the cleaning plant where lots of water is available to rinse it. How often should this be done? Perhaps every five to ten years, although of course in some homes or offices the rugs should be cleaned perhaps every two or three years.

REPAIR - This is a most neglected area in the preservation of a valuable Oriental rug. People paint their house and make repairs to it but many let their rugs go until they are nearly beyond repair or at least require many hours of work and large sums of money to be made presentable again. If in good condition as to side wrappings, overcasting of the ends, absence of wrinkles or buckles and so on, an Oriental rug will not require much if any repair during the first fifteen to twenty years' use. Sides and ends do not become worn overnight. It is only after sides and ends need refinishing that problems occur. Complete neglect of a rug with edges and ends in bad condition can cause irreparable damage to the rug and result in a substantial decrease in its value.

SIZING, FINISHING - Make sure your rug lies flat on the floor. Don't let the salesman tell you large wrinkles will walk out. We block and size nearly every rug we sell and in almost every case they stay flat. Unfortunately, many stores sell rugs just as they are unbaled without proper servicing. Just about every new rug requires some little work on edges or ends. On some expensive Iranian types like the Tabriz we often have to put a complete new overcasting on the sides–a considerable expense but one that is necessary if the rug is to give trouble free service.

MOTH PROOFING - Your Oriental rugs should be moth proofed occasionally, perhaps once a year. While we moth proof every rug we sell and while the treatment probably lasts longer than a year we urge you to spend an hour each year or so and moth proof each rug you own. Commercial moth proofing solutions are widely available from large department or hardware stores. Sprayed on with an aerosol can or an old fashioned flit gun, moth proofing is quickly applied. Be sure to apply the solution on the underside of the rug for an area about a foot wide in from the edge. This is the area of the rug most likely to be attacked by moths or carpet beetle larvae crawling in under the rug. Be aware that most moth proofing solutions are insecticides in a petroleum solvent base. The insecticide is a poison and the solvent is flammable, so use and store the moth proofing with care!

Most of the moth damage that comes to our attention involves rugs owned by elderly couples who had given the rugs little attention for many, many years. Sometimes rugs will be damaged in storage if they are not clean, moth proofed, and properly wrapped when put away. No good rug should be stored in a basement where it may be damaged by moisture or in a barn or garage where squirrels or mice may nest in the rug.

PADDING UNDER RUG - We recommend a sponge rubber, rubberized felt, or dense plastic foam pad under every rug--even the thickest. It not only increases the life of any rug, but it helps keep the rug in place and is so delightful under foot.

CARE FOR YOUR VALUABLE ORIENTAL RUGS!

CHAPTER SEVENTEEN

DEMISE OF USED RUG SALES

Years ago the "Used Rug Sale" was often advertised by large department stores. This type of sale finally fell into disrepute after hundreds of used rug sales over a period of many years. In a typical ad for one of these sales there would be listed a few hundred rugs by size and price. In the first years of these sales some 25% of the rugs were actually "used" rugs. The rest were really new. In a short time very few of the rugs advertised for each sale were used rugs. Many customers, very knowledgeable about Oriental rugs, reported they searched in vain for the one used rug among the many listed at the sale. Yet the ads continued--"Used Rug Sale"--with lots of different types of rugs, each followed with an 'E' indicating "excellent condition." Colonel Jacobsen vividly recalls seeing an importer ask the largest promoter of such sales, "How do you have the nerve to list all these rugs as 'used'?" The promoter stepped on a new rug at his feet and with a wave of his hand exclaimed, "Now it is a used rug." This was apparently the case with most rugs advertised. Not only were most of the "used" rugs actually new, but few were of really first quality for the type. Rug sale promoters more often than not assembled numbers of rejects from the wholesale market to be disposed of at their "sales."

Why did such advertisements bring so many sales and become so successful over such a period of years? To some buyers "used" gave the impression of antique or semi-antique rugs and rugs with soft old colors. In fact the ads sometimes claimed that the rugs for sale actually came from private estates. To other buyers the "used rug" meant lower prices. Unfortunately there were usually few real bargains at these sales, even when the rug was actually used or worn. Obviously you can fool some of the people some of the time, but it is doubtful if this used rug sale gimmick will ever again be as successful again on a large scale. Still, be aware of the game and be certain you know what you are buying.

CHAPTER EIGHTEEN

ONE MAN'S OPINION

For the last several years Iranian rugs have almost ceased to be a factor in the new rug market. Unless radical changes come to Iran this situation will continue for years to come. Rugs are still woven in the cities, villages, and countryside but the organization of buyers and sellers who brought rugs to market and arranged for their export disappeared when the Shah left Iran in 1979. Because of the great difficulty in dealing with the new bureaucracy of the Iranian government, few if any foreign buyers have been able to travel and buy in Iran in recent years. The Iranian government has tightened currency controls which has had the effect of making Iranian rugs more expensive. Most of the Iranian rugs found in the wholesale markets today are pieces which were brought from Iran years ago. Today most rugs come from India, China, Pakistan, Turkey, and Rumania. These are all areas where good rugs are still available at reasonable prices and it is from these countries that most rugs will come for the foreseeable future.

CAUCASIAN AND TURKOMAN RUGS FROM CENTRAL ASIA - Sooner or later it may be that the United States and Russia will reach enough agreement to permit the normalization of trade with each other. When this happens it will bring United States' customs duty on Russian rugs into line with duty on rugs from other countries and will open the door to the import of Caucasian types and Turkoman types from southern Russia. These pieces will compete with geometric types from Turkey, Pakistan, and Iran and competition like this always helps the rug buyer.

RUGS FROM CHINA - Duty has declined on rugs from mainland China and there is healthy competition right now among importers who have brought in large quantities of Chinese rugs and carpets. I do not think that there are great numbers of Chinese rugs to be sold year in and year out but they will always be popular with some buyers. Much depends upon the actions of the Chinese government who can change rug prices to us at will making their rugs more or less expensive as they see fit. Rug sales to the West are an important source of foreign credits to the Chinese, however, and so they are likely to continue to encourage dealers to buy. Of course, the Chinese still face the problem of competition from less expensive rugs in Chinese design woven in India.

COLLECTING ORIENTAL RUGS TODAY - If money was not important and I wanted rare, antique Oriental rugs, I would pay the price for the best rugs in the best condition I could find. This does not mean, however, that I would pay any price for a particular rug. I would not buy the badly worn rare antique unless the rug was just too beautiful to pass. I would not buy the average worn antique--the Hamadan, Herez, Karaja, and others. I would buy the super example of one of these types. By "super" I mean that the rug would have to have the finest quality wool–like panne velvet--and have beautiful colors because these are not, as a class, collector's types. And I would not hesitate to collect some of the best new Orientals available today. As one who has been an antique rug man most of my life, having sold nothing but antique and semi-antique Orientals during my first thirty-five years in business, and one who has furnished rare rugs to many collectors, many museums, and to scores of historical homes, I may sound like a turncoat when I say that if I were buying rugs for my own use today I would choose some of the choice new Orientals in preference to most of the antiques to be had. I do feel that there are new rugs available in today's market that will be judged outstanding in years to come.

If I could afford it I would buy a fine Nain or Isphahan from Iran but I would also consider several of the types from India in Iranian designs. From Pakistan I would select several of the choice and fine rugs in Tekke and Salor designs. From Turkey there are the traditional types like prayer Ghiordes, Kula, prayer Ladik, Melez, Bergamo, and other types. I would select also some of the prayer Kazaks, Shirvans, and Kabistans made in Turkey. I would certainly select some of the Jaipur area rugs from India in the Shirvan design. One could have the foundation for an excellent collection with these and a few other types.

Not only would rugs like these have beauty and quality but if one speculates about future value it seems to me these types would have a better chance to appreciate than those rug varieties that are already so very much overpriced.

RECAPITULATION - Even with the changes in the rug situation in the last decade there is hope for the future. There is a good supply of real Oriental rugs to choose among--rugs as choice and beautiful as those available ten, twenty, or fifty years ago. In my opinion, there is a better selection of rugs in scatter sizes and carpets up to 10 x 14 ft. available today than we have had from Iran during the past fifteen years. The rugs from Rumania use excellent designs and soft, rich colors (new rugs from Rumania often look more like antique Persian rugs than new rugs from Iran). I am also delighted and surprised each succeeding month over the designs, quality, and beauty of the new Turkish rugs coming on the market. So far, most are small to 6 x 9 ft. or perhaps 7 x 10 ft. in size. Let's hope that these rugs will keep their old authentic designs, the good wool, and the nice colors of those we have seen to date. We hope that the weavers will not let the great demand for Orientals lead them into reducing quality in favor of volume as they did after World War I. Pakistan continues to supply many quality Oriental rugs to America and Europe. Most are Bokharas and rugs in geometric designs. At an honest price there is no better value than one of these better made Bokharas. The right ones are magnificent--actually more beautiful than old Bokharas from Central Asia, rugs now seldom available.

India has become the largest producer of Persian-like Oriental rugs. But with some 600 million people and some 20 million born every year they still have only about 100,000 weavers in the Mirzapur district (Varanasi). Perhaps there are 50,000 weavers elsewhere in the country. Training centers have been set up for weavers by the government but the number being trained each year is not great. Having switched from making Savonneries to weaving Persian design rugs they have become the main supplier of moderate priced rugs. We continue to be pleased and delighted by the increasing variety and quality of the rugs from India.

Already the Indian made Herez, Serapi, Abadeh, Sarouk, Joshigan, Karaja, Sarabend, and others offer much better value than the comparable Iranian type. For example, the Iranian Sarabend has priced itself out of the market, at least in my judgment. Some native Persian dealers will still declare their loyalty to this rug but anyone with two eyes and a hand to feel the quality will buy the Sarabend from India at half the price of the Iranian Sarabend. The new Iranian rug is brighter and actually not as beautiful as the one from India. In the case of this design as with others there are many qualities of Sarabend rugs woven in India today. The least expensive is a good looking rug at one-fourth to one-third the price of the Iranian version. One should carefully inspect the rug and evaluate the price asked; as always country of origin is no guarantee of quality.

India continues to have some problems in meeting demand. It is necessary for us to visit India regularly in order to inspect our goods, examine new designs and encourage producers, but still disruptions in supply can occur. Rug weaving is a very important source of foreign credits to the Indian economy and so the government does try to help resolve problems. If they are effective in encouraging weaving, India will remain the largest producer of hand woven Orientals in the world.

Afghanistan has sent thousands of rugs to America in recent years. If the fighting stopped today there would still be a serious question about the future of Afghan rugs. Damage done to Afghan society and culture by years of warfare cannot be made to disappear. With whole villages destroyed and thousands made refugees one wonders how long the traditional ways can survive. We would also expect to see an effect on some of the Pakistani types eventually, as Afghan refugees settle in adjacent areas of Pakistan.

PERSONALITIES - I had expected the first edition of my UPDATED GUIDE to be my last effort as an author but old habits stay with me and it is difficult to resist the urge to tell people a little more about Oriental rugs. I have always tried to simply set down the facts about rugs as I know them and over the years the response to my books has been extremely gratifying.

I would especially like to thank all those people who over the years have taken the time to write or call or to visit us in Syracuse. Many of my friends ask why I stay active in the business. My answer is that I like people and especially the people I have met through the rug business. When in Syracuse I would be lost if I did not have an office to go to and people to meet who come to buy rugs from us. I stay active in my senior years because I feel that the officers and employees of our business want me to stay and feel that I am still needed. I am glad to say that they now own a substantial part of the business and that Charles W. Jacobsen, Inc. will continue to serve rug buyers for many years to come.